Calamity in Carolina

THE BATTLES OF AVERASBORO AND BENTONVILLE, MARCH 1865

By Daniel T. Davis
and Phillip S. Greenwalt

EMERGING CIVIL WAR SERIES

Chris Mackowski, series editor
Daniel T. Davis, chief historian

Also part of the Emerging Civil War Series:

The Aftermath of Battle: The Burial of the Civil War Dead
   by Meg Thompson

Bloody Autumn: The Shenandoah Valley Campaign of 1864
   by Daniel T. Davis and Phillip S. Greenwalt

Bushwhacking on a Grand Scale: The Battle of Chickamauga, Sept. 18-20, 1863
   by William Lee White

Dawn of Victory: Breakthrough at Petersburg, March 25-April 2, 1865
   by Edward S. Alexander

Fight Like the Devil: The First Day at Gettysburg, July 1, 1863
   by Chris Mackowski and Daniel T. Davis

Grant's Last Battle: The Story Behind the Personal Memoirs of Ulysses S. Grant
   by Chris Mackowski

Hurricane from the Heavens: The Battle of Cold Harbor, May 26-June 5, 1864
   by Daniel T. Davis and Phillip S. Greenwalt

The Last Days of Stonewall Jackson: The Mortal Wounding of the Confederacy's Greatest Icon
   by Chris Mackowski and Kristopher D. White

No Turning Back: A Guide to the 1864 Overland Campaign
   by Robert M. Dunkerly, Donald C. Pfanz, and David R. Ruth

A Season of Slaughter: The Battle of Spotsylvania Court House, May 8-21, 1864
   by Chris Mackowski and Kristopher D. White

Simply Murder: The Battle of Fredericksburg, December 13, 1862
   by Chris Mackowski and Kristopher D. White

Strike Them a Blow: Battles Along the North Anna, May 21-25, 1864
   by Chris Mackowski

That Furious Struggle: Chancellorsville and the High Tide of the Confederacy, May 1-5, 1863
   by Chris Mackowski and Kristopher D. White

To the Bitter End: Appomattox, Bennett Place, and the Surrenders of the Confederacy
   by Robert M. Dunkerly

Calamity in Carolina

THE BATTLES OF AVERASBORO AND BENTONVILLE, MARCH 1865

By Daniel T. Davis
and Phillip S. Greenwalt

EMERGING CIVIL WAR SERIES

SB
Savas Beatie
California

ISBN-13: 978-1-61121-245-7

Library of Congress Control Number: 2014958714

First edition, first printing

Published by
Savas Beatie LLC
989 Governor Drive, Suite 102
El Dorado Hills, California 95762
Phone: 916-941-6896
Email: sales@savasbeatie.com
Web: www.savasbeatie.com

Savas Beatie titles are available at special discounts for bulk purchases in the United States by corporations, institutions, and other organizations. For more details, please contact Special Sales, P.O. Box 4527, El Dorado Hills, CA 95762, or you may e-mail us as at sales@savasbeatie.com, or visit our website at www.savasbeatie.com for additional information.

DAN: *For my grandfather, the first Daniel T. Davis*

RMC US Navy
World War II
Korea
Nov. 2, 1918—Mar. 11, 1982

PHILL: *For my sister and brother, Adrienne and Patrick*

Table of Contents

A reconstructed cabin that once stood on the grounds of the Lebanon Plantation at Averasboro now stands in the Chicora Cemetery. (kb)

List of Maps

Maps by Hal Jespersen

Acknowledgments

Many individuals assisted us in bringing this work to publication, not the least of which is the editor of the Emerging Civil War Series, Chris Mackowski. Chris is a great friend, and his guidance has helped us grow as historians and writers. He also contributed an appendix to this work. Kristopher D. White, emeritus editor and co-founder of the Emerging Civil War blog, has also been instrumental in our careers.

We are blessed to work with a great group of historians at the Emerging Civil War. Christopher L. Kolakowski graciously took time away from his busy schedule to review the manuscript. Ashley Webb wrote a wonderful appendix on the impact on civilians of Sherman's maneuvers. Derek Maxfield loaned us a picture of Sherman's HQ in Savannah. Eric J. Wittenberg, an authority on Civil War cavalry operations, provided excellent insight on some intricate pieces related to Averasboro and Bentonville. Eric also provided an introduction to Wade Sokolosky, an authority on Civil War North Carolina. Like Eric, Wade was a patient sounding board. Similarly, Rob Orrison introduced us to Donny Taylor, the Historic Site Supervisor at Bentonville. Donny took time away from preparing for the Sesquicentennial to contribute a critical appendix on the preservation efforts at Bentonville. Always a joy to work with is Bert Dunkerly. He pried himself away from *To the Bitter End* to write an appendix on a key aspect of the battle of Bentonville.

Derrick Brown and Amanda Bentley, also of Bentonville, helped us with identifying battle sketches. Derrick was also kind enough to act as a guide to the Army of Tennessee earthworks. David Hall gave an excellent tour of the Harper house.

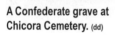

A Confederate grave at Chicora Cemetery. (dd)

The redoubtable John Coski of the Museum of the Confederacy sent us a copy of one of his ancestor's letters who fought at Bentonville.

Mark A. Moore, who helped bring the battles of Averasboro and Bentonville to life through his beautiful maps, wrote a superb foreword.

We would also be remiss if we didn't express a deep debt of gratitude to Theodore Savas and Sarah Keeney of Savas Beatie, LLC. Once again, they have helped bring one of our manuscripts to fruition. The incomparable Hal Jespersen worked with us to build a superb set of maps.

DAN: My beautiful wife Katy continues to be my foundation for all that I do. She accompanied me on battlefield trips to Averasboro and Bentonville. I cherish every moment with her. Also joining us were my brother, Matt, and his fiancée, Candice. Katy and I wish them all the best as they embark in a new life together. To my parents, Tommy and Kathy Davis, who instilled in me at an early age a love for the Civil War. "What's the idea, Porter?!" Lastly, to all of my family and friends, I can't thank you enough for your ongoing support.

PHILL: To my soul mate, best friend, travel partner, and battlefield companion, my wife Adel. She has made me a greater person, and her continued support, not to mention her willingness to allow me to turn a drive back from a vacation into a research trip to Averasboro and Bentonville just shows how lucky I am. To my parents, Stephen and Melanie, who fostered from an early age my interest in American history and continue to provide support and accompaniment on many a battlefield visit. To all the friends and family, too numerous to count, who have provided an encouraging word, support, or just checked in to see how the project was coming along— thank you!

A monument to Federal units that fought at Bentonville sits on the battlefield. (dd)

PHOTO CREDITS:
Gene Adcock (ga)
Battles & Leaders (b&l)
Katherine Bowen (kb)
Daniel Davis (dd)
Matthew Davis/Candice Coleman (md/cc)
Phillip Greenwalt (pg)
Harper's Weekly (hw)
Library of Congress (loc)
Chris Mackowski (cm)
Derek Maxfield (dm)
North Carolina Division of Archives and History (ncdah)

For the Emerging Civil War Series

Theodore P. Savas, *publisher*
Chris Mackowski, *series editor*
Daniel T. Davis, *chief historian*
Sarah Keeney, *editorial consultant*
Kristopher D. White, *emeritus editor and co-founder*

Maps by Hal Jespersen
Design and layout by Chris Mackowski

Confederate graves stand near the Bentonville Battlefield Visitor Center. (cm)

Foreword

By Mark A. Moore

Civil War military campaigns, especially those involving large armies that traveled hundreds of miles to achieve their objectives, were complex events that are difficult to fully understand without in-depth study.

For historians, from the most erudite academicians to knowledgeable researchers of every stripe, such campaigns offer seemingly endless avenues of study. From civilian politicians who influenced the course of military actions to the common soldiers who served and died to achieve political objectives, the elements that build the larger narrative are multifaceted. Ideology, command structure, leadership, conflicting personalities, social interaction, logistics, morale, geography, weather, and good or ill fortune—all of these aspects had a direct impact on the course of military events. Historians can spend years studying a single campaign, gaining a wealth of knowledge in the process, while still not being able to answer every question that arises from their research. Imparting the knowledge gained, in writing, is a challenge at any level.

Where does the general reader begin? There are many overview studies of the war. But what if a casual reader is interested in a specific campaign or battle? Does the reader dive right in to the existing scholarship? In many cases, the answer is yes—because for certain battles and campaigns, that is all that is available with any degree of accuracy. If general readers are interested in anything beyond Gettysburg or the larger battles

A number of Confederate soldiers who died at Bentonville are buried in a cemetery adjacent to the battlefield visitor center. (dd)

and campaigns, their options diminish as they look for knowledgeable overviews of other aspects of the war.

The Emerging Civil War series seeks to address this deficiency by offering an introductory bridge between the reader's interest and the deeper scholarship available. The series paints in broad strokes while striving to offer enough detail and insight to foster understanding, to stoke the interest of readers, and steer them toward deeper knowledge.

With *Calamity in Carolina*, authors Daniel Davis and Phillip Greenwalt tackle the final days of the Civil War in North Carolina, and the last big battles between the armies of William T. Sherman and Joseph E. Johnston— an epic and poignant campaign. The Confederate capital of Richmond, Virginia, was on the verge of collapse and a junction of the armies of Johnston and Robert E. Lee seemed all but probable as Sherman tightened the noose in North Carolina.

In addition to the history of events that occurred 150 years ago, the authors provide information on places to visit and driving tours to help readers connect the past with the public history facilities that currently interpret it. Further context is offered through a series of informative sidebars. Appendices provide analysis of the effect of Sherman's March on civilians; Mower's Charge and Hardee's counterattack; Maj. Gen. Joseph A. Mower; the eventual surrender at Bennett Place; the postwar friendship between Sherman and Johnston; and the all-important preservation of the battlefield at Bentonville. Lastly, a useful "suggested reading" section provides readers with a list of more in-depth studies of the campaign and battles.

Sherman deemed the March to the Sea "child's play" when compared to his Campaign of the Carolinas. Johnston likened Sherman's veteran soldiers to the armies of Julius Caesar. The stakes were high with no shortage of drama. These pages are a good place to start learning about it.

MARK A. MOORE *is a cartographer and the author of* The North Carolina Civil War Atlas: The Old North State at War *and* Moore's Historical Guide to the Battle of Bentonville.

"Concentrate all available forces
and stop Sherman."

— Robert E. Lee to
Joseph E. Johnston
February 22, 1865

Prologue

FEBRUARY 1865

In March 2010,
a monument was dedicated
to Confederate Gen. Joseph
Johnston on the Bentonville
battlefield. The plot of land
where the monument stands
was donated by a local
landowner and is maintained
by the Sons of Confederate
Veterans. Crafted by Carl
Regutti, the total cost of
the monument was around
$100,000. A "Walk of Honor"
leads from the parking
area to the monument. The
bricks in the walk bear the
names of men who fought
for the Confederacy. The
only other monument
to Johnston stands in
Dalton, Georgia, where the
general established his
headquarters in the winter of
1863-1864. (dd)

Joseph E. Johnston was back in his element, back in the arena he had dedicated most of his adult life to. Sitting astride his stallion, the salt-and-pepper haired general cast his glance toward the soldiers marching through Charlotte, North Carolina. The tattered remnants of homespun Confederate uniforms hung from their shoulders like Spanish moss, yet the men, many of them barefooted, shuffled proudly by their commander. With their battle-scarred standards waving above them, the remnants of the Army of Tennessee erupted into "three cheers," which one participant remembered was given "in a very joyous tone" and was in the "manner of great satisfaction." A Confederate veteran remembered the cheering as a sign "of the great satisfaction."

That was one of the reasons Johnston was back in command: he had the confidence of the army—or at least the portion of the army that had not been killed or maimed at Franklin and Nashville late in 1864.

General Robert E. Lee, now commander of all Confederate forces, had brought Johnston back from administrative exile, where he'd been banished the previous summer. Johnston had been relieved of command of the Army of Tennessee during the Atlanta campaign for a perceived lack of aggression. Johnston had languished in the months since, and during that time, the Confederacy's fortunes had taken a steep dive. Lee, now under siege around Richmond and Petersburg, Virginia, by Lt. Gen. Ulysses S. Grant, needed experienced help.

Confederate cavalry delayed the Union advance in the fields around the Johnston monument during the opening stages of the fighting at Bentonville. The Bentonville Battlefield Visitor Center sits in the distance. (dd)

The plaque of the Johnston statue lauds "Old Joe" as the "Defender of the Southland to the End." (pg)

"J. E. Johnston is the only officer whom I know who has the confidence of the army," Lee told Confederate President Jefferson Davis. Davis and Johnston had a troubled history together, but Lee, who had graduated from West Point with Johnston in 1822, trusted him implicitly.

Johnston, always a stickler for his reputation, had initially greeted the news of his restoration with skepticism. He believed he was restored to command in order to allow Davis to blame him for the ultimate Confederate defeat, which Johnson felt was surely coming. But when Johnston learned that it had not been Davis but Lee who'd restored him, the old soldier moved with more alacrity. His old friend and fellow Virginian was a man he had "loved and admired . . . more than any man in the world."

Lee confirmed that he did not expect miracles from Johnston's meager forces. "I will rely on you and we will both hope for the best," Lee wrote to him. Although sanguine about the prospects, Johnston vowed "that Knight of old never fought under his King more loyally than I'll serve under General Lee."

The Virginian would need more than bravado in his new post. Marching toward him from the south were the blue legions of Maj. Gen. William Tecumseh Sherman.

After having completed his "March to the Sea," from Atlanta to Savannah, Sherman had turned north, striking into South Carolina. North Carolina was his next target, and Sherman was aiming for a rendezvous with Union forces coming westward from the coast. He had overwhelming strength compared to the meager remnants of the Army of Tennessee, garrison troops, home guard, cavalry, and even teenagers that Johnston could manage to scrape together to face the Union juggernaut.

Lee's directive to Johnston was to concentrate those forces "and drive back Sherman."

Johnston had met Sherman once before, back in northwest Georgia. There, Johnston had fought primarily on the defensive in the hopes of wearing Sherman down by inflicting high casualties.

Major General William Tecumseh Sherman was one of Johnston's chief antagonists during the war and a dear friend after. (loc)

Could something similar work in North Carolina in 1865?

Johnston was also a realist and knew that he did not have the numbers to fight Sherman on equal footing. To comply with these orders, Johnston would have to go on the offensive. If he could consolidate his forces and wait for an opportunity where the advantage was in his favor, Johnston could then rely on his troops to pounce.

These thoughts and his memories must have raced through Johnston's mind on that cold February day as he took the measure of his men and considered his options.

These men were still with their colors; these men still believed; these men could be trusted. Back with them, Johnston felt at home again.

Maybe he could, indeed strike a blow to the Federals as Lee envisioned.

Johnston had his orders. He would certainly try.

War is All Hell

CHAPTER ONE

FEBRUARY-MARCH 1865

A cool air greeted the congregation as they stepped from the Episcopal Church. The sound of the tolling bells followed the group as they dispersed through Savannah, Georgia. Reaching into his coat, Maj. Gen. William Tecumseh Sherman pulled a short cigar from his pocket. It was Christmas, and the recently sung carols still echoed in his ears as he made his way across the evergreen-lined street. Puffing furiously, his thoughts were focused forward—not just on the street but in a much larger sense. Reaching the house of a Mr. Charles Green, Sherman removed the now-reduced nub from between his teeth and discarded it as he stepped inside.

His mind constantly at work, it was not hard for Sherman to appreciate how far his armies had come on their march through Georgia—or just how much farther he planned to take them. After a campaign that had lasted through the spring and summer of 1864, Sherman captured the vital enemy rail center of Atlanta on September 2. In an attempt to draw the Federals out of the city, Lt. Gen. John Bell Hood's Army of Tennessee struck out to the north. Hood hoped to damage Sherman's supply lines and ultimately take many of his hardened veterans back to their native state. Although Sherman detached troops to deal with Hood—and he himself left the city with them on pursuit—he had no intention of abandoning his hard-won prize to chase the Rebels. Instead, "Uncle Billy," as he was known to his men, was formulating a daring plan.

Sherman wrote to his close friend and general

Fort Pulaski's guns protected Savannah. (pg)

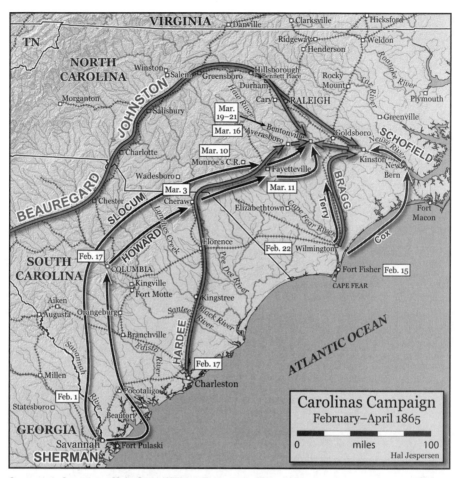

CAROLINAS CAMPAIGN—**Maj. Gen. William Tecumseh Sherman began his advance north from Savannah on February 1, 1865. His intent was to "punish South Carolina," and his men burned a wide swath through the state in retaliation for its decision to be the first state to secede in 1861. As Union troops moved in from the coast, Gen. Joseph Johnston assembled a force to slow Sherman. Johnston would engage the Yankees in North Carolina at Averasboro and Bentonville.**

in chief, Lt. Gen. Ulysses S. Grant, on October 9: "I propose . . . that we strike out with our wagons for Milledgeville, Millen and Savannah. Until we can repopulate Georgia, it is useless for us to occupy it; but the utter destruction of its roads, houses and people will cripple their military resources. . . . I can make this march and make Georgia howl!"

Grant initially balked at the idea, wishing that his close friend from the west would deal with Hood first, but his reservations were overcome by his trust in Sherman's judgment. He directed Sherman to "go on as you propose" on November 2.

Two weeks later, Sherman left Atlanta with 62,000

"Uncle Billy" vowed to "make Georgia howl." (loc)

men. Doing what Hood could not, he cut his own supply lines, along with communication with the outside world, and headed his columns for the coast. In less than a month, the Yankees had tramped through the state and had reached the outskirts of Savannah. The capture of Fort McAlister south of the city forced the Confederates to evacuate on the night of December 20. Two days later, Sherman sent a telegram to President Abraham Lincoln: "I beg to present to you as a Christmas-gift the city of Savannah."

Sherman's armies wreaked havoc on their "March to the Sea." By destroying infrastructure, he aimed to take away the South's ability to wage war. (loc)

Following the capture of Savannah, Grant intended to bring Sherman to Virginia where he was battling Robert E. Lee for control of the cities of Richmond and Petersburg. Word of Hood's defeat by Maj. Gen. George Thomas at Nashville on December 16, and the estimated two months it would take to transfer Sherman by sea to Virginia, caused Grant once again to change his mind. "I did think the best thing to do was to bring the greater part of your army here, and wipe out Lee,"

Grant wrote. "The turn affairs now seem to be taking has now shaken me in that opinion. I doubt whether you may not accomplish more toward that result where you are . . . I want to get your views about what ought to be done."

Sherman used the Charles Green residence as his Savannah headquarters while his armies occupied the city. (dm)

The night before, on Christmas Eve, sitting at his desk inside the Green house, Sherman answered his commander. He had thought the reply over for so long and so well that, in his mind, it appeared as clear as daylight: From Savannah, he would take his armies north, through the Carolinas.

Writing to Grant, Sherman said, "I left Augusta [Georgia] untouched on purpose, because the enemy will be in doubt as to my objective point . . . whether it be Augusta or Charleston [South Carolina]. . . . I will then move either on Branchville or Columbia . . . breaking up in our course as much railroad as possible. . . . I would then favor a movement direct on Raleigh [North Carolina]."

Although preparatory movements began in the middle of January, the weather delayed Sherman's columns from beginning their trek north until February 1, 1865. Marching through the first state to secede from the Union—also infamous as the state where the opening shots had been fired—the Federals entered the state capital of Columbia on February 17. That evening, high winds fanned flames from cotton bales lit by withdrawing enemy forces, newly freed slaves, and Union soldiers. The winds carried the fire throughout Columbia, and the city burned.

"The morning sun of February 18th rose bright and clear over a ruined city," Sherman recalled. "About half of it was in ashes and smoldering heaps."

*   *   *

The Federal marches through Georgia and the Carolinas were revolutionary in their concept. According to the military conventions of the day, war was to be made

The Green house offered Sherman a much-needed respite after weeks on the march. (loc)

between opposing armies. William Tecumseh Sherman took this idea one step further. Instead of focusing on enemy forces, he turned his efforts toward his enemy's logistics and the civilians supporting them. Essentially, Sherman's men lived off the land, gathering their food and supplies from homes and farms along their route.

At a gathering of Union veterans after the war in Columbus, Ohio, Sherman told the crowd, "There is many a boy . . . who looks on war as all glory, but boys, it is all hell." Uncle Billy had released his own brand of hell on the Southern populace in what has become known as "total war."

In early February 1864, roughly a year before he struck out from Savannah, Sherman had an opportunity to test this theory of total war. He led 27,000 soldiers east from Vicksburg to Meridian, Mississippi. Stripping the country bare of sustenance along the way, upon his arrival, his men wrecked the town's rail lines. This expedition helped convince Sherman that his new way of making war could be effective.

While on the march, the Yankee soldiers would strip down to only the bare necessities: a canteen, haversack, tin cup, and cartridge box with 40 rounds of ammunition. Some men chose to carry an additional 20 rounds in their pockets. Any personal belongings were rolled up in a blanket and tied diagonally across their shoulders. These flying columns were to move as quickly as possible, averaging around 15 miles a day. While on the march, foragers from each company were sent out to gather the day's provender.

An aspect of Sherman's strategy was to convince

the citizenry that with such a large force moving through the South, further resistance on the battlefield would be futile. "It is but right that these people should feel some of the hardships of war," one Union soldier wrote. "[T]hey will better appreciate peace when it does come, and be not so ready to rush wildly into the same vortex again."

Indeed, Sherman's armies resembled the population of a large city moving through the South. "The march through Georgia has been called a grand military promenade, all novelty and excitement," a Massachusetts soldier said. "But its moral effect on friend and foe was immense. It proved our ability to lay open the heart of the Confederacy."

The same could not be said of South Carolina as the seasoned campaigners struggled in the chilly weather through the swamps of the Low Country, which winter rains had turned to lakes and roads to bottomless trails of muck. The elements would not deter the Federals, though, for they were on the same ground that gave rise to secession and the cursed war. One Union officer described the Federal march through South Carolina as a "stubborn wrestle with the elements . . . where . . . the indomitable will . . . won a physical triumph." Destruction now accompanied the foraging parties. A Buckeye soldier remembered "not a house or fence was left standing, along our march" and that the columns were followed "by the dark cloud of smoke made by burning cotton gins and outbuildings."

Vengeance fueled the Federals as they trudged through the Carolinas, their movement reminiscent of the great Roman legions.

"When I learned that Sherman's army was marching through the Salkehatchie swamps," recalled Confederate Gen. Joseph E. Johnston, "making its own corduroy road at the rate of a dozen miles a day or more and bringing its artillery and wagons with it, I made up my mind that there had been no such army in existence since the days of Julius Caesar."

*   *   *

Sherman did not dally long in the charred remains of South Carolina's capital. "Having utterly ruined Columbia," the column continued onward.

The movement resembled that of another army through the Carolinas some 85 years before. Lord Charles Cornwallis' British force had cut their own supply lines in order to speedily pursue Continental forces through the interior of the colonies. Eventually, the exhausted redcoats were forced to withdraw to Wilmington to refit and resupply. Sherman would be faced with a similar situation as he marched ever farther from Savannah.

On March 11, he reached Fayetteville, North Carolina. Sherman wrote proudly that "I took up my quarters at the old United States Arsenal, which was in fine order and had been much enlarged by the Confederate authorities, who never dreamed that an invading army would reach it."

There in Fayetteville, Sherman would give his men a few days of hard-earned rest before opening the final chapter of another epic march.

In Savannah

Sitting on one of the islands at the entrance to Savannah is Fort Pulaski, now run by the National Park Service, but the concept of the fort dates back to the War of 1812 when its construction was ordered by President James Madison.

Construction, however, did not begin until 1829, and a 22-year-old West Point graduate by the name of Robert E. Lee arrived shortly thereafter to oversee the building of the fort. Four years later, the fort was named after Kazimierz Pulaski, a Polish officer who joined the American cause during the Revolutionary War.

After Georgia seceded and joined the Confederacy, Southern troops garrisoned the brick-and-mortar fortification. The fort would stay under Southern control until April 11, 1862, when it was surrendered to the Federals.

The surrender of the fort demonstrated the effect of early technological advances in weaponry during the American Civil War. The longer-range rifled artillery used by the Union during a 30-hour bombardment had caused severe damage to the outer walls. The Confederate cannon—all of which were less-accurate smoothbores—could not reach the approximately four- to five-mile range of the besieging Union artillery pieces.

The fort then began a second phase of its Civil War history as a final destination for the Underground Railroad. Later, it morphed into a prison. After the war,

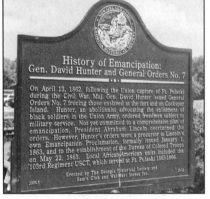

After the surrender of Ft. Pulaski in 1862, Union Gen. David Hunter issued a general order permitting free blacks to serve. Although revoked, the order served as a prelude to Lincoln's more comprehensive Emancipation plan. (pg)

In June 1861, Confederates in Charleston, South Carolina, placed imprisoned Union officers in range of Federal guns to deter bombardment of the city. To counteract the measure, Secretary of War Edwin Stanton placed a similar number of Confederate soldiers within range of Rebel guns on Morris Island, outside Charleston. In October 1864, Lt. Gen. William Hardee ordered the removal of the Union prisoners. The Federals then transferred 600 Confederates to Fort Pulaski, where half of them eventually died. These Prisoners are known as the "Immortal 600." (pg)

the fort continued as a military prison and actually held a few former Confederate cabinet members.

Venturing into the town, multiple sites still stand that have Civil War connections. Most notable is the home where William T. Sherman established his headquarters in December 1864, the Green-Meldrim house, which is now a museum.

Laurel Grove Cemetery, one of two impressive, well-manicured Civil War cemeteries. It includes the grave site of Confederate general Lafayette McLaws, who fought in the campaign that culminated at Bentonville. Other Civil War luminaries include Moxley Sorrel, staff-officer to James Longstreet and historian of the war whose posthumously published account is still well received, and Francis Bartow, a Confederate general killed at First Manassas.

The second of Savannah's cemeteries, Bonaventure Cemetery, sits on the grounds of a former plantation of the same name. The cemetery has been a highlight for tourists for a century and a half with its notable internments and natural beauty. Alexander Lawton, who is best known for serving as quartermaster general for the Confederacy, is interred there. Another interesting burial is that of Hugh Weedon Mercer, who also rose to the rank of brigadier general. He died in Baden-Baden, Germany, in 1877—and certain accounts still hold that he is buried there. However, other records suggest he was reinterred at Bonaventure in 1879, so a gravesite and headstone marks his possible resting place in this cemetery, too. Lastly, Josiah

Tattnall, Jr., who commanded the famed C.S.S. *Virginia* ironclad after that ship's engagement with the U.S.S. *Monitor*—and the commander who ordered the *Virginia* scuttled when Norfolk, Virginia, was abandoned—is also buried in Bonaventure.

The reverse side of Lafayette McLaws' grave says, "I fought not for what I thought was right but for principles that were right." (pg)

Approximately 21 miles from downtown Savannah sites Fort McAllister, located in Richmond Hill. The fort, which is now a Georgia State Park, initially blocked Sherman's entrance into the city.

To visit these points of interest:

Fort Pulaski
National Monument
US Highway 80 East
Savannah, GA 31410

Fort McAllister State Park
3894 Fort McAllister Rd.
Richmond Hill, GA 31324

Green-Meldrim House
14 West Macon Street,
Savannah, GA 13401

Laurel Grove Cemetery
(Note: There is a North and
a South Laurel Grove Cemetery,
but they are in the same geographic area.)
North: 802 West Anderson St.
Savannah, GA 31415
South: 2101 Kollock St.
Savannah, GA 31415

Savannah Visitors
Information Center
301 Martin Luther King, Jr. Blvd.
Savannah, GA 31401

"Uncle Billy" and His Armies

CHAPTER TWO
FEBRUARY-MARCH 1865

Piles of bricks crashing to the ground rent the air as the Yankees destroyed the old U.S. arsenal in Fayetteville—along with local iron foundries and cotton mills. With sounds of the crumbling buildings ringing in his ears, Harvey Reid, an infantryman from the 22nd Wisconsin wrote to his parents. "This campaign has far exceeded in hardship and somewhat in danger the Savannah one," he told them, "but still this army is in excellent health and spirits. It is probable that we shall remain here but a very short time."

Reid was not far off in his guess. Sherman did not plan on staying long. The energetic Westerner was anxious to continue onward.

Sherman had always been energetic. Born in Lancaster, Ohio, he was known to his family and friends as "Cump"—a shortening of his middle name, Tecumseh. At the age of nine, Sherman was sent to live with neighbors following the death of his father. His adopted father was Thomas Ewing, a future United States senator. With Ewing's assistance, Sherman entered the United States Military Academy at West Point and graduated in the Class of 1840. Missing the fighting in Mexico, Sherman instead served, ironically, in various posts in the South.

In 1850, he married his foster sister, Ellen. Resigning from the army three years later, Sherman attempted to run a bank in San Francisco. When it failed, he tried law—with little success. When South Carolina seceded in December 1860, Sherman was the Superintendent of

The remains of the
U.S. Arsenal in Fayetteville,
North Carolina (dd)

the Louisiana State Seminary of Learning and Military Academy, now Louisiana State University.

Leaving the post, he was appointed colonel of the 13th U.S. Infantry and fought at First Manassas. Promoted to brigadier general late in the summer of 1861, he transferred to Kentucky. There, Sherman constantly worried about a lack of manpower and an impending enemy offensive. These concerns reached his superiors and the Northern press. Relieved from command and branded "insane" by reporters, Sherman was sent to St. Louis.

Major General Henry Halleck, commander of the Department of Missouri, plucked Sherman from obscurity over the winter, and in February 1862, Sherman found himself back in Kentucky supporting Brig. Gen. Ulysses S. Grant's operations against Ft. Donelson. Soon thereafter, he was back in the field, commanding one of Grant's divisions at Shiloh.

Promoted to major general in May, Sherman served as military governor of Memphis and fought at Arkansas Post. Under Grant's eye, the tall and lithe man with red hair and beard commanded a corps in the campaign that resulted in the capture of Vicksburg, closing the Mississippi for the Confederacy. In the fall of 1863, Sherman followed Grant to Chattanooga, Tennessee, and helped lift the siege of the city. When Grant was promoted to lieutenant general and commander of all Union forces in the spring of 1864, Sherman assumed command of the Union armies in the West.

Despite his battlefield success, Sherman had other storms to endure, including the loss of two children. His son William died of dysentery prior to Chattanooga at the age of nine. "People write to me that I am a great general and if I were to come home they would gather round me and play music," he wrote in November 1864 to his son Tommy. "That is what people call fame and glory, but I tell you I would rather come down quietly and have you and Willy meet me at the car than to have the shouts of the people."

In December, shortly after reaching Savannah, Sherman learned of the death of his 10-month-old son, Charles, from a newspaper.

*   *   *

Sherman's surrogate family was the one he rode at the head of through Georgia and the Carolinas. They

affectionately called him Uncle Billy, these men of the Army of Georgia and the Army of the Tennessee—a complex mix of men and officers who had seen action in both the Eastern and Western theaters.

Major General Henry Slocum commanded the Army of Georgia. The New Yorker had commanded the old XII Corps in the Army of the Potomac, most notably at Chancellorsville and Gettysburg. After the disaster at Chickamauga, the XII Corps the XI Corps had been sent to Chattanooga and consolidated as the XX Corps, but Slocum was relegated to duty guarding a railroad. During the Atlanta campaign, Slocum was on duty in Vicksburg.

Internal army politics brought Slocum back to the army. Major General Joseph "Fighting Joe" Hooker, disgusted that he had not received a promotion he felt entitled to, resigned. That created a vacancy at the head of XX Corps, which Sherman called on Slocum to fill.

Slocum's army consisted of the XX Corps and the XIV Corps, which was commanded by Maj. Gen. Jefferson Columbus Davis. Consisting of men from the Army of the Cumberland, these veterans had fought at Corinth, Perryville, and Stones River. Their commander was a seasoned officer. A veteran of the Mexican War, Davis had performed well during the Civil War. He is best known for having shot and killed his former commanding officer, Brig. Gen. William Nelson, following a quarrel early in the war. Brigadier Generals William Carlin and James Morgan and Maj. Gen. Absalom Baird led Davis' three divisions.

Major General Alpheus Williams led the XX Corps, which had been fighting under Slocum since his days in Virginia with the Army of the Potomac. Before serving with Sherman, these Easterners had faced

Major General Henry Slocum (left), an old veteran of the Eastern battles, commanded the Army of Georgia. The army consisted of the XIV Corps, led by Maj. Gen. Jefferson Columbus Davis (center), and the XX Corps, under Maj. Gen. Alpheus Williams (right). (loc)

Known as "Old Prayer Book," Maj. Gen. Oliver Otis Howard (left) commanded the Army of the Tennessee. Major General John Logan (center) led the XV Corps, and Maj. Gen. Frank Blair (right) led the XVII Corps. (loc)

Judson Kilpatrick's recklessness in battle contributed to his lack of military success and earned him the nickname "Kil-Cavalry." (loc)

down Gen. Robert E. Lee and Stonewall Jackson with mixed results. Williams had three dependable division commanders in Brig. Gens. Nathaniel Jackson, John Geary, and William Ward.

Sherman's second army, the Army of the Tennessee, was led by Maj. Gen. Oliver Howard. Deeply religious and ardently abolitionist, Howard had lost an arm at Seven Pines. Later, he turned in lackluster performances commanding the XI Corps at Chancellorsville and Gettysburg—yet his career managed to survive.

Major Generals John "Black Jack" Logan and Frank Blair, Jr., led Howard's two corps, the XV and XVII, respectively. Logan's nickname was derived from his dark eyes and hair. Active in the Democrat Party prior to the war, he had served with the army since the battle of Belmont in 1861 and had receive the Medal of Honor for his actions at Vicksburg. Logan's divisions were headed by Maj. Gens. Charles Woods, William Hazen, John E. Smith and John Corse.

Like Logan, Blair was also a veteran of the Western campaigns and one of Sherman's favorite officers. He could depend on the leadership of Maj. Gen. Joseph Mower, Brig. Gen. Manning Force, and Maj. Gen. Giles Smith to command his divisions.

By the early spring of 1865, the Army of the Tennessee had compiled a splendid combat record, fighting at Fort Henry, Fort Donelson, and Shiloh and capturing Vicksburg and Atlanta.

Sherman had a lone cavalry division accompanying his armies under Maj. Gen. Judson Kilpatrick. Kilpatrick was a West Pointer and a known womanizer. He was a veteran of cavalry actions in Virginia, but questionable decisions at Gettysburg in July of 1863 and during a

Federals marched past the burning buildings of McPhersonville, South Carolina, in early February, 1865 (top), then later crossed the Salkehatchie River (below). (loc)

raid on Richmond in the spring of 1864 had gotten him transferred west of the Appalachians.

On the march, Sherman divided his armies. Slocum constituted the left wing and Howard the right. This assignment not only gave the Yankees the flexibility to move rapidly across multiple roads and to deceive the Rebels of any intended destination, it provided for a greater expanse of land from which the men drew supplies.

While marching in separate formations provided decided advantages, it potentially played into the hands of his enemy, too. The

columns would be able to support each other, but by and large, they would be isolated from each other, making them vulnerable to individual attack or even delay. That, in turn, could be problematic because Sherman could not remain stationary for an extended period in open country lest his men run out of food.

Sherman planned to resupply his armies at the railroad junction of Goldsboro, North Carolina. Although the line from Wilmington was severely damaged, the Union Navy, under Rear Admiral David Porter, could unload supplies onto trains at Morehead City for transport inland. Major General John Schofield's XVIII Corps was transferred from Tennessee to reinforce Maj. Gen. Alfred Terry in securing the town ahead of Sherman's arrival.

For several days, Sherman's armies laid waste to the Confederate means to wage war in Fayetteville. Then, on March 15, they marched over the Cape Fear River on pontoon bridges and set out again.

Time was crucial.

TOP: The Saluda River in South Carolina provided another barrier for the Army of the Tennessee. (loc) BOTTOM: XIV Corps marched through Fayetteville, North Carolina. (b&l)

At Fayetteville

An artist's rendering of the Fayetteville Arsenal during the war shows one of the octagonal guard towers (top); today, foundational remains mark the spot (bottom). (b&l; dd)

The shadows of Sherman's visit to Fayetteville can still be seen today. One can view the remains of the U.S. Arsenal destroyed by the Union army on the grounds of the Museum of the Cape Fear River Historical Complex.

Construction began in the late 1830s and lasted for fifteen years. When North Carolina seceded, a local militia unit took control of the complex. Equipment captured at Harper's Ferry was used during the war to make weapons and ammunition. Sherman would use it as his headquarters while his army encamped around the city.

All that remains today are the foundation stones. The outline of a "Ghost Tower" has been reconstructed at the facility's northwest corner and dominates the surrounding area. Originally, the tower was one of four constructed to guard the arsenal.

The museum interprets the history of the Cape Fear

Erected in 1928 by the North Carolina Historical Commission and the J.E.B. Stuart Chapter of the United Daughters of the Confederacy, a monument for the Fayetteville Arsenal stands outside the entrance to the Museum of the Cape Fear River and Arsenal Grounds. (dd)

River and its impact on the surrounding area. There is a Civil War exhibit upstairs. On display is a Henry Rifle purportedly captured at the battle of Monroe's Crossroads.

Another area of interest is the Cross Creek Cemetery. Established in 1785, the most prominent landmark in the cemetery is the Confederate War Monument. The monument was dedicated in 1868 through funds raised by a former Confederate nurse, Anna Kyle. It is surrounded by the graves of North Carolinians who served in the Confederate army.

To reach the cemetery from the museum, turn left and proceed to the first stoplight and turn right onto Hay Street. Proceed on Hay Street through historical Fayetteville. At the first traffic circle, you'll notice the Market House. Union and Confederate

RIGHT: A Confederate War Monument stands in the Cross Creek Cemetery. (dd) OPPOSITE: To help give visitors an idea of the immensity of the Arsenal, a "Ghost Tower" has been constructed on the grounds. It stands today on the site of the northwest tower, which was built between 1839-1840. Octagonal in shape, the tower was three stories tall. (dd)

soldiers skirmished through this area as the Federals entered Fayetteville.

Continue on Hay Street. At the next traffic circle (the second traffic circle), bear to the right and proceed on North Cool Spring Street past the city's visitor center. After .2 miles, you will reach the cemetery, which is on the right.

To visit these points of interest:

Cape Fear River Historical Complex
801 Arsenal Avenue
Fayetteville, North Carolina 28305

Fayetteville City Visitor Center
245 Person Street
Fayetteville, North Carolina 28301

The Last Rally
of the Western Confederates
CHAPTER THREE
FEBRUARY-MARCH 1865

The troops that Gen. Joseph E. Johnston witnessed during his late-February review were the proud remnants of the Army of Tennessee. When the much-maligned Lt. Gen. John Bell Hood navigated his defeated army away from the twin disasters of Franklin and Nashville the previous November, the men moved south into northern Mississippi.

The rank-and-file had numbered approximately 18,000 men at that time, but over the course of winter, the army dwindled even further. Troops were pulled to different posts, including Mobile, Alabama; some were allowed to leave on furlough; Georgians were returned to their native state. Desertions ran high. Many of the men that left on furlough turned their temporary absence into permanent leave, especially after the disastrous late autumn campaign.

One of the reasons for the large number of desertions was the uneven distribution of furloughs. Hood allowed the Mississippi soldiers to return home but, according to one of the division commanders in the Army of Tennessee, "the failure to extend to the troops of Georgia, Alabama, and South Carolina . . . the same indulgences as had been granted to those of Mississippi, gave much dissatisfaction." This prompted "large numbers to leave the ranks" as the army settled into their encampment.

Hood was officially relieved from command of the Army of Tennessee on January 23, 1865. General

A monument to William Taliaferro's division stands on the Averasboro battlefield. Taliaferro's command was part of the patchwork Johnston attempted to assemble to stop Sherman. (dd)

When facing a foe of superior size, Gen. Joseph Johnston preferred to operate defensively and wait for a chance to strike—a strategy that served his armies effectively but one that did not sit well with offense-minded Southern people and political leadership. (loc)

Richard Taylor assumed temporary command of the army while Confederate President Jefferson Davis cast about for a new permanent replacement. He loathed to reappoint Joe Johnston, with whom he'd had a stormy relationship, but Robert E. Lee, as general in chief of all the armies, insisted.

The forces left at Johnston's disposal were completely spread out. The largest component, the Army of Tennessee, had men stretched from Tupelo, Mississippi, to Charlotte, North Carolina. When orders came through to move those scattered remnants of the army to the Carolinas, the senior corps commander, Lt. Gen. Alexander. P. Stewart, was placed in charge of the move. Still, the men largely lacked the necessities needed for active campaigning, missing accoutrements, wagons, rifles, and artillery.

By late February, Stewart's men converged on Charlotte, which was believed by Confederate authorities to be the next objective of Sherman's northward movement. Johnston awaited them there. As the grizzled veterans marched through the city, "the army was cheered" to be under his command again, one of them later remembered. Their numbers may have been drastically reduced—the entire army was now the size of a single corps from the previous year—but Johnston needed these men to form the backbone of "The Last Rally" of the Confederacy, one soldier wrote.

Thirty-five hundred of the men belonged to the corps of Lt. Gen. Stephen Dill Lee, the youngest man to hold that rank in Confederate service. Lee had been wounded in mid-December during the retreat from Nashville and would not return to command until March. In the meantime, his command was led by Carter Stevenson, a major general from Fredericksburg, Virginia, who had seen extensive service with the Army of Tennessee. His men had arrived in time to try and stop Sherman's legions in South Carolina, but due to their small number did not do more than harass the northern-advancing Union soldiers.

Twelve hundred more soldiers constituted Stewart's command. The Tennessean had commanded a corps in the army, but now the total number of men following him was equivalent in size to a regiment from the beginning of the war.

Lt. Gen. Alexander Stewart (left) and Lt. Gen. William J. Hardee (right). Stewart, a professor before the war, was known for his general bookishness, while Hardee literally wrote the book on infantry tactics widely used by both sides in the war, *Rifle and Light Infantry Tactics for the Exercise and Manoeuvres of Troops When Acting as Light Infantry or Riflemen.* (loc)

The last contingent from the Army of Tennessee was under corps commander Maj. Gen. Frank Cheatham. Around 1,900 men still marched with the heavy-drinking, hard-fighting Tennessean.

Even if all the infantry arrived, Johnston was deeply concerned about the number of men who lacked rifles. Many had discarded their firearms since their last engagements the previous fall.

"In my opinion," Johnston wrote to Lee, "these troops form an army too weak to cope with Sherman."

*　*　*

Heading north at the same time, by rail and by foot, was another contingent of Confederates under a face familiar to Johnston: Lt. Gen. William J. Hardee. Since leaving the Army of Tennessee after the unsuccessful battle of Jonesboro, around Atlanta, in early September, Hardee commanded the Department of South Carolina, Georgia, and Florida from Savannah, Georgia. Sherman's approach in December had forced Hardee to evacuate and head to Charleston.

With the evacuation of Charleston, which was ordered by Gen. P. G. T. Beauregard on February 15, Hardee organized the remnants of the various troop commands into an active force. This interesting collection of heavy artillerymen, a depleted brigade from the Army of Northern Virginia, Georgia militia, and garrison troops numbered fewer than 5,000 effectives. "[M]ost of them had been for a long time accustomed only to garrison duty," one Confederate noted. Hardee admitted that many "had never seen field service."

Some of the troops that marched north with Hardee had at one time worn Union blue and were known as "galvanized Yankees." This term applied to

Lt. Gen. John Bell Hood succeeded Johnston to command the Army of Tennessee during the Atlanta Campaign. Hood's failed campaign in the early winter of 1864 wrecked the army. The following year, Johnston would call the remnants eastward to serve once more. (loc)

Maj. Gen. Lafayette McLaws had run afoul of Lt. Gen. James Longstreet after the Knoxville campaign in the fall of 1863. When his court-martial for inefficiency was overturned by procedural reasons, McLaws nonetheless left the Army of Northern Virginia. Since late 1863, he had seen extensive service in defense of his native state. (loc)

captured Union soldiers who had volunteered to serve the Confederacy to escape the confines of a Southern prison. Hardee had firsthand experience with this type of soldier and had advised through official channels that enlistment should be stopped. With the Confederacy needing every available man, Hardee's recommendation was ignored, and now, ironically, he was stuck with the turncoats as he trudged north.

As Hardee's column fled west then north from Charleston, his command had to outpace the advancing Yankee soldiers if they were to have any hope of completing a rendezvous with Confederate forces in North Carolina. One thing that evened the race between Hardee and Sherman was the weather. This allowed valuable Confederate supplies to be moved by railroad out of Sherman's clutches, but it also caused severe problems for men of both forces marching through the deepening mud and flooded creeks and streams.

Many of Hardee's men did not make it to the border with North Carolina. By the end of the month, a "great many desertions from the command" had taken place.

But Hardee did successfully—and by the narrowest of margins—make it to North Carolina, providing a few thousand extra soldiers for Johnston's army. They would play an instrumental role in the opening act of the campaign.

What Hardee lacked in frontline soldiers he made up for with a motley collection of general officers that had seen a variety of duties during the war.

One of Hardee's divisions was led by Georgian Maj. Gen. Lafayette McLaws. The other division was led by Virginian William Taliaferro. Taliaferro had once served with Lt. Gen. Thomas "Stonewall" Jackson and later led the Confederacy to victory at the largest land battle in Florida at Olustee in February 1864.

Hardee had been forced to consolidate his last division, under Maj. Gen. Ambrose Wright, with McLaws' and Taliferro's when Wright took a leave of absence to serve in the Georgia legislature.

*　*　*

As Johnston gathered the remnants of the Army of Tennessee in Charlotte, approximately 200 miles to the east, other Confederate forces were on the move. Another veteran unit, an infantry division under Tar Heel Maj. Gen. Robert Hoke, was slowly backtracking

Two former officers of Robert E. Lee's Army of Northern Virginia, Maj. Gens. Robert Hoke and Daniel Harvey Hill, would fight in Johnston's hodge-podge army. Hoke had developed a reputation as a dependable fighter, as had Hill—who had also developed an unfortunate reputation as someone who didn't get along well with his superiors. (loc)

from the coast. Unfortunately, with Hoke's infantry came Gen. Braxton Bragg, who had rushed from his job as a military advisor to Jefferson Davis to help with the defense of his native North Carolina. In the interim, Bragg had attached himself to Hoke's forces. As welcome as Hoke and his infantry would be, the addition of Bragg, a previous army commander, would serve as a detriment.

On March 8, Bragg showed he still lacked battlefield acumen by turning another potential victory into defeat—an act that would foreshadow future actions. Hoke had engaged Maj. Gen. John Schofield's Federals at Wise's Fork, near Kinston, North Carolina. Although not present at the battle, Johnston who had by then relocated to a more central location in North Carolina at the town of Smithfield, reacted to news from the engagement and rushed in reinforcements. The troops, contingents of the Army of Tennessee at his current disposal, were led by Maj. Gen. Daniel Harvey "D. H." Hill, who had come north from a department command to be of service to Johnston. These men allowed Bragg to send Hoke's veterans into Schofield's left flank where Hoke's men captured an entire Union regiment.

Then, Bragg intervened and slammed shut any possibility of a Confederate victory. Instead of continuing the offensive, Bragg halted the advance and sent Hill with a force to stall a supposed Union threat. The threat never materialized, thus ending the fighting on the first day.

After more ineffectual skirmishing, including an unwise attempt to assault the fortified Union position on March 10, Bragg ordered a withdrawal. His return to field command began much like it had ended in late 1863, with defeat won from the jaws of victory.

Bragg then marched west to a rendezvous with Johnston. In the process, Bragg created an unenviable position for Johnston simply by virtue of being around:

Braxton Bragg's service in the Mexican War pegged him as a promising officer. He would eventually rise to the top echelons of Confederate command, where he proved to be one of the most controversial generals of the war. (loc)

At the outbreak of the war, Wade Hampton was reputedly the richest man in the Confederacy. A South Carolina planter, Hampton, unlike many of the men he would fight alongside, was not a West Point graduate. Using his own funds to raise a mixed unit of infantry and cavalry, known as the Hampton Legion, Hampton took his men to Virginia. In July 1862, Hampton took command of a cavalry brigade and became one of Maj. Gen. J. E. B. Stuart's most aggressive and dependable subordinates. Severely wounded at Gettysburg, Hampton later returned and took over command of Robert E. Lee's cavalry when Stuart was killed at Yellow Tavern in May 1864. In January 1865, Hampton was dispatched to North Carolina to help contend with Sherman's armies. (loc)

Bragg was a Davis confidante and a former commander of the Army of Tennessee.

If having Bragg around did not make the situation more stressful for Johnston, the Virginia commander also had to deal with D. H. Hill, another strong-willed officer and one of the most intense fighters in Confederate service to ever attain the rank of lieutenant general. Hill had shown his mettle leading troops in combat on multiple occasions. One of his finest days was September 14, 1862, when he fought a superb delaying action at South Mountain during the Antietam campaign.

Unfortunately, Hill also had the same mentality on the battlefield as in camp, often sparring with fellow officers. His prickly temperament led to his reassignment from the Army of Northern Virginia. Later, after a fall out among the Confederate officer corps following the battle of Chickamauga in September 1863, Hill was again left without a command. He served in lesser department commands until early 1865 when he was attached to Johnston's consolidating forces.

Besides the foot soldiers making their way to North Carolina, approximately 6,000 cavalrymen also reported for service with Johnston's forces. They were commanded by Lt. Gen. Wade Hampton, who had requested a reassignment to South Carolina to defend his home state and so had left the Army of Northern Virginia in January 1865. Major General Joseph Wheeler's horsemen added to Johnston's cavalry force.

On March 10, Hampton struck Union cavalry under Maj. Gen. Judson Kilpatrick west of Fayetteville, North Carolina. The Confederates scored a successful surprise when the Rebels thundered into the slumbering Union encampment. Some participants remembered the battle as "Kilpatrick's Shirttail Skedaddle" because of the precipitous flight the Union cavalry commander made in his undershirt.

The Federals responded and eventually pushed back the Confederates to regain their camps. The Southern assault gave time for Hardee's infantry to cross the Cape Fear River and continue toward Johnston's concentration. The Rebel cavalry had proven, if just for a day, it still had some bite.

And so Johnston pulled to him everyone he could—garrison soldiers, militia, skeleton-sized units from the two principle Confederate field armies, and a varied assortment of generals that had been cast off from other posts, overlooked or just simply left without commands.

With this miscellaneous collection of troops, the old soldier, "with no other hope than of [obtaining] favorable terms of peace," set about consolidating his forces and preparing to give battle to Sherman.

* * *

William T. Sherman's combined force numbered 60,000 soldiers. Major General John Schofield, moving inland from the coast, added another 20,000. Sherman was intent on a junction with Schofield and reaching a secure supply line. If these two Union forces were to converge, though, Johnston, with approximately 20,000 troops at his disposal, would face overwhelming odds. The Virginian predicated his whole campaign on stopping this.

He had previously admitted that he thought it was "too late" for him to be expected to "concentrate troops capable of driving back Sherman." Johnston's only hope was to consolidate his scattered forces and then look for an opportunity to attack when Sherman's armies were divided and isolated.

Johnston had chosen Smithfield for a junction of his own. The town sits some 45 miles northeast of Fayetteville, North Carolina; 30 miles southeast of the state capital of Raleigh; and just under 25 miles from Goldsboro.

After arriving in Smithfield, Johnston began preparations for action once his forces consolidated. He needed to develop Sherman's intentions—to anticipate what Sherman would do was essential. Johnston needed time. Would Sherman oblige him? Or would the metaphorical house of cards Johnston was delicately constructing in central North Carolina with his various combined commands be brushed aside before he even had a chance to stop the Yankees?

Those were the dilemmas that faced the career military man. One issue that was assuaged for Johnston happened when he rode into Smithfield and received a spirited welcome from the Southerners gathering there. The Virginian was cheered by the rank and file, with the cheers from the Army of Tennessee being the most spirited. Even former officers voiced their pleasure and "expressed . . . the joy the Army of Tennessee manifested" for Johnston.

As the number of soldiers continued to increase at Smithfield, Johnston could only hope that his chances of success would also.

Hampton's chief subordinate was Maj. Gen. Joseph Wheeler. Wheeler was a veteran of Shiloh, the Kentucky Campaign, Chattanooga, and Atlanta. Years after the war, despite having been a Confederate office, he would be commissioned a major general of U.S. Volunteers and commanded troops during the Spanish-American War. (loc)

The Battle of Averasboro

CHAPTER FOUR

MARCH 15-16, 1865

Rains had turned the North Carolina roads to muck. Such conditions did not deter Uncle Billy. In the past, his men had marched in conditions much worse than what they would encounter north of Fayetteville.

For the final leg of the march, Sherman decided to send Howard and the Army of the Tennessee toward Goldsboro. To deceive the Confederates, who Sherman knew were lurking in the area, Slocum would take the Army of Georgia north on a feint toward the state capital of Raleigh. Once he reached the vicinity of Averasboro, he would abruptly turn east and march to Goldsboro through a small town known as Bentonville. Sherman decided to ride with Slocum.

"Kilpatrick's cavalry rode on in advance," a soldier in Slocum's army wrote, "we following as fast as the wretched roads would permit. The recent rains compelled us to build corduroy much of the way."

Sometime around three in the afternoon, the Yankee cavalry ran into Confederate skirmishers. One man from the 9th Michigan remembered that the regiment was "briskly engaged." These skirmishers were only the outliers of an impressive Confederate battle line.

After abandoning Fayetteville in the wake of the Yankee march, William Hardee's corps withdrew north to protect the route to Raleigh. He placed his units at the junction of the Raleigh and Goldsboro Roads to block and ascertain the direction of the Union advance. With the position Hardee chose, Sherman would have no choice but to engage the Confederates.

If Hardee did not make a stand near Averasboro, he might not have had a force to fight with. Desertions and

The First Confederate line on the Averasboro battlefield. A monument to Union soldiers from the XX Corps who fought in the battle stands at the far end of the earthworks. (md/cc)

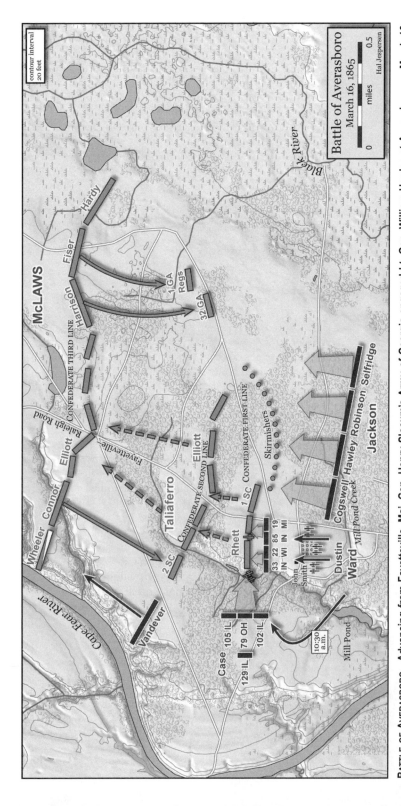

BATTLE OF AVERASBORO—Advancing from Fayetteville, Maj. Gen. Henry Slocum's Army of Georgia engaged Lt. Gen. William Hardee at Averasboro on March 16. Hardee assembled his men in three lines, with Maj. Gen. Lafayette McLaws holding the strongest, and fought what is known as a defense in depth, steadily slowing the Union advance. A flanking Federal brigade broke the first line, and the sheer weight of numbers overwhelmed the second before Confederate cavalry reinforcements and darkness brought the advance to a halt in front of the third line.

After leaving Fayetteville, Sherman's armies marched past Old Bluff Church, founded in 1758. His men camped around the church prior to the battle of Averasboro. (dd)

recalls by state governors had started to sap the strength of the command.

On March 15, the Union advance ran into the Confederates. By this time, Hardee had chosen a defense-in-depth: three parallel lines, each within supporting distance of each other, blocked the road. Colonel Alfred Rhett's brigade of South Carolinians manned the first line. Several hundred yards behind Rhett was the brigade of Col. Stephen Elliot. Backstopping Elliot was Lafayette McLaws' division.

Hardee, the well-schooled military tactician, might have thought he could win another improbable victory in the Carolinas similar to Daniel Morgan's victory at the battle of Cowpens during the American Revolution.

As the skirmishing began, a small party of Federals led by Capt. Theo Northrop, Kilpatrick's Chief of Scouts, encountered a group of Confederate officers. When challenged, Northrop found that it was none other than Colonel Rhett and members of his staff. Northrop had somehow slipped through the Confederate skirmish line.

A sketch of the battle of Averasboro. (loc)

An interesting exchange then took place. When approached by two horsemen, Northrup was asked by one of the riders the location of a certain Confederate force.

Northrop responded by saying, "You will have to come with us."

This drew the anger of one of the gray officers. "Do you know who you are talking to?" he bristled. "I am Colonel Rhett?" The South Carolinian tried to draw his revolver, but a member of the Union party quickly thrust a carbine to his head. That ended Rhett's attempt to achieve the upper hand.

"Well, this is cool," Rhett said as he gave up his sidearm and surrendered. That evening, Rhett dined with Sherman, Slocum, and Davis.

As the next morning dawned, sparring between both sides resumed. The "opposition continued stubborn," Sherman later wrote. Colonel William Butler, now heading Rhett's command, put up such stiff defense that Slocum decided to deploy the divisions of Nathaniel Jackson and William Ward to engage the Rebels.

"We moved forward to the attack," an officer in the 2nd Massachusetts remembered. "The enemy gave us a hot reception which we returned with a storm of lead. It was a wretched place for a fight. At some points we had to support our wounded until they could be carried off, to prevent their falling into the swamp water."

Unable to break Butler's line head on, Sherman told Slocum "that a brigade should make a wide circuit by the left, and . . . catch this line in flank." Colonel Henry Case was chosen for the assignment. He wrote that his men "sprang forward with alacrity, with a deafening yell, and the moment they emerged from the thicket in sight of the enemy they joined in a destructive fire upon their ranks. . . . [T]he enemy . . . completely taken by surprise, fled precipitately in the utmost confusion."

The spelling of Brig. Gen. William Taliaferro's last name belies its pronunciation: "TOL-e-ver." His rank belies his reputation as a hard-nosed fighter: run-ins with former superior Stonewall Jackson led to his banishment west and stymied his career. (loc)

With Butler's men streaming headlong for the rear, the Union advance continued on to Elliot's line. Here, the Yankees kept up such a "continual and sharp . . . fire" that one South Carolinian remembered "the smoke settled among the undergrowth and under the treetops in such quantity that a foe could not even be seen a short

A cannon outside the Averasboro Battlefield Museum faces south toward the third Confederate line. (pg)

distance away." Overwhelming numbers eventually forced Elliot's men to retreat and rejoin McLaws.

As the Federal advanced continued toward McLaws, Hardee deployed the newly arrived cavalry under Joe Wheeler to protect his right flank. The deployment was fortuitous, as the Yankees were attempting to replicate Case's early flanking maneuver. This time, Brig. Gen. William Vandever's brigade of James Morgan's newly arrived division was attempting to turn the enemy line. "[A]fter crossing a deep and difficult ravine, I advanced my line as far as the ground would permit . . ." Vandever wrote. "I succeeded in pushing across . . . two companies of the Sixtieth Illinois . . . and three companies of the Seventeenth New York; but they had to remain under cover . . . being too close to the enemy's works . . . the firing all along my line was heavy and protracted."

The Confederate line proved to be too strong for the Yankees, though. With darkness and heavy rains, the Union advance ground to a halt on McLaws' front. After showing "more pluck than we have seen in them since

Taliaferro's men held the first two defensive lines, including these earthworks along the first line. (pg)

Atlanta," according to a Union veteran, the Confederates had demonstrated they still had fight left in them. All told, combined losses for both sides exceeded 1,100.

Militarily, Hardee had turned in a textbook-style delaying action. Judiciously that night, he abandoned his works and withdrew to join Johnston. It would not be long, however, until "Old Reliable" and his men would meet the Yankees on the field of battle again.

Defense in Depth

In the early 1850s, with the endorsement of then Secretary of War Jefferson Davis, Hardee authored a manual on military drill. At Averasboro, Hardee applied his knowledge of tactics and employed what is known as a defense in depth. The tactic was often utilized by troops with little combat experience. Many of the men under Hardee's command had served most of the war defending the city of Charleston, South Carolina, and had not campaigned actively in the field. Additionally, Hardee was facing of nearly two to one odds. As such, he decided to defend an area between the Cape Fear River on the west and the Black River on the east. This would allow Hardee to place his men in a compact area, making it easier to maneuver his smaller force.

The basic concept of the tactic calls for troops defending a position to form in as many parallel lines as practicable, in this instance three. The first line is to hold on as long as possible, before falling back to the second line. This position, now reinforced by men from the first, continues to delay the oncoming enemy. When it becomes futile to sustain this position, the second line

retreats to the last and strongest position. Ideally, the third line is made up of the more experienced soldiers. By the time the attacker reaches the final line, they are exhausted and thus at the mercy of a counterattack by the combat hardened veterans.

Parts of the first (opposite), second (top), and third (bottom) Confederate lines at Averasboro. (dd)

When Slocum's men reached McLaws' position, daylight was growing dim and if the Yankees wished to renew the offensive they would have to wait until the following morning. Hardee would not give them the opportunity; he had held up Sherman's advance for a full day, allowing Johnston to consolidate his forces.

Marching to Battle

CHAPTER FIVE

MARCH 17-18, 1865

"All of our troops behaved extremely well," Henry Slocum proudly wrote following the engagement at Averasboro. The day after the battle, Slocum's wing resumed its march toward Goldsboro. Howard, unaffected at all by the engagement, also continued his movement toward the town. The incessant rain and resulting mud slowed the Federals, though making the advance "most wearisome." One officer remembered the roads were "nearly impassable" resulting in much "laborious marching."

While the Yankees continued their efforts in corduroying the roads, one Union soldier recalled the foragers "pushing ahead . . . in the keen quest of something to eat, had provoked a skirmish with a detachment of the . . . enemy." Quickly discerning the "affair was too large . . . to handle . . . they galloped away in another direction to hunt for pigpens and smokehouses." These Rebel detachments encountered by the blue foragers were keeping a close eye on Slocum's advance.

In the wake of Slocum's column, meanwhile, Hampton's butternut troopers had been riding along the Goldsboro Road. On the evening of March 17, the South Carolinian bivouacked at the Cole Plantation. Like Hardee's action the day before, Hampton was now executing the textbook role of cavalry: screening, skirmishing, and gathering intelligence. As the day wore on and Hampton continued to contest the Federal march, he became convinced that Sherman might be headed for Goldsboro. This discernment would have a profound impact on Confederate strategy.

Around midnight, Hampton received a dispatch

Swamps dot the land between the Averasboro battlefield and the Yankees' ultimate destination of Goldsboro. (dd)

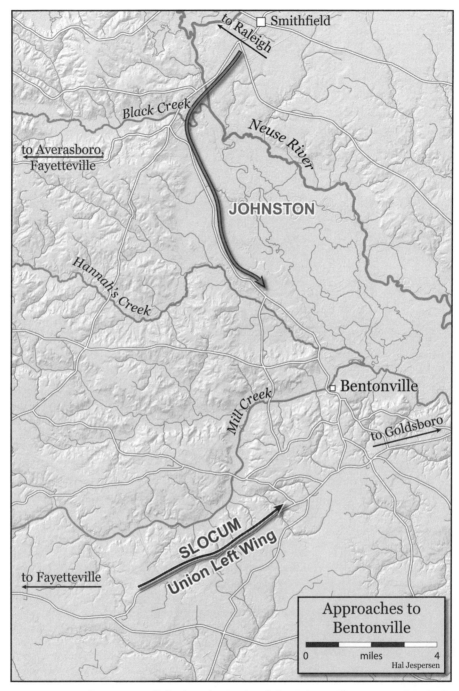

APPROACHES TO BENTONVILLE—Following the battle of Averasboro, Sherman continued his advance toward Goldsboro. Meanwhile, Johnston was finally ready to attack the Federals with his concentrated force. Johnston set off from Smithfield in an attempt to head off Henry Slocum's wing and destroy it while it was isolated from the rest of Sherman's forces.

Johnston's army marched along this road—the Devil's Race Track Road (facing south)—from Smithfield to reach Hampton's position below Bentonville. (dd)

from Johnston, inquiring as to the feasibility of assaulting one of Sherman's wings. The cavalry chief replied, outlining the disposition of the opposing forces. He then suggested to Johnston that "the point at which I was encamped was an admirable one for the attack . . . and that I would delay the enemy as much as possible so as to enable us to concentrate there."

Hampton's selection of the Cole property was tactically sound. The property was situated near the intersection of the Smithfield Road and the main route between Averasboro and Goldsboro. Use of the Smithfield Road would give the Confederates easy access to block the Federal march. North of the house, the ground rose into a slight but heavily wooded plateau.

Hampton recognized that the slope would not only mask any movements to his position but offered the perfect location in which to conceal infantry for an assault on Union soldiers moving along the road below.

Upon receiving the dispatch, Johnston "determined . . . to attack. Bragg and . . . Stewart . . . were directed to march through Bentonville and encamp between that point and the [Averasborough] Road, and Lieutenant General Hardee . . . was instructed to join them."

Johnston would come to call this force the Army of the South. It would be up to his conglomerate of Hardee's troops, the remnants of the Army of Tennessee, Hoke's division, and Hampton's cavalry to defeat Sherman in North Carolina.

The next morning, Hampton moved out with Brig. Gen. George Dibrell's cavalry division to contest the Yankee advance. Hampton remembered they met the enemy and "skirmished until the afternoon, when I was pressed back by the force of numbers to the crest of a wooded hill which overlooked a very large field that I had selected as a proper place for the battle. . . . [I]t was near sunset when the enemy moved on this position and recognizing its strength . . . withdrew after a rather feeble demonstration." One trooper summed up the South Carolinian's stance perfectly: "Old Hampton is playing a bluff game, and if he don't mind Sherman will call him."

That night, Hampton rode to Johnston's headquarters to complete the plans and deployments for the following day's engagement. Hampton had performed superbly throughout his Virginia service earlier in the war. Now, his actions of monitoring and delaying Slocum's advance had set the stage for Johnston, like a coiled snake, to strike a blow at Uncle Billy.

The coming days would define the worth of Hampton's efforts and whether Johnston could stop Sherman.

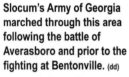

Slocum's Army of Georgia marched through this area following the battle of Averasboro and prior to the fighting at Bentonville. (dd)

Built by William Hastings in the mid-1850s in Smithfield, this house was the shared headquarters of Joseph Johnston and Braxton Bragg. It was here that Johnston planned to strike the Union army as it advanced to Goldsboro. Originally constructed to the rear of the Johnston County Courthouse, the house was moved in 1941, and then moved again, to its current location, in the 1960s. (dd)

Bentonville Opens

CHAPTER SIX

MARCH 19, 1865

Rising early on the morning of March 19, an air of complacency accompanied William Sherman as he prepared for his daily responsibilities. He wrote afterwards "all signs induced me to believe that the enemy would make no further opposition to our progress, and would not attempt to strike us . . . while in motion." With that idea in mind, Sherman bid adieu to the Army of Georgia and rode toward Howard's Army of the Tennessee. It would not be long before events on Slocum's front would shatter his overconfidence.

As Hampton turned in a masterful delaying action on March 18, Confederate infantry tramped toward Bentonville. Due to faulty maps, though, the hike by some Southern foot-soldiers was longer than expected. Hardee's maps showed the distance to the North Carolina town as approximately 12 miles from their encampments. The rank-and-file would find out the distance was a little longer—closer to 20 miles. This might not seem like much of a distance, but the Rebels were marching on reduced rations.

Still, the espirit de corps was high for the combined elements of Johnston's Army of the South. By dawn on March 19, most of the Confederates—except Hardee's men, who were still five miles away—were in position along the line at Bentonville.

A large portion of the credit for Johnston's plan of attack goes to Wade Hampton. Hampton had made good use of his time during his stay at the Cole house, making himself familiar with the heavily wooded area around his headquarters. Hampton suggested using Hoke's Division as the main blocking force, positioning

The grave of Sam Thornton, one of the postwar owners of the Harper House, stands near the Bentonville Battlefield Visitor Center. Colonel George Dibrell's cavalry delayed the Union infantry through the fields where Thornton's grave is located. (dd)

it astride the Goldsboro Road, which the Yankees would be using for their approach. Deploying on Hoke's right, and contorting the line in a 45-degree shift to follow the terrain, would be Stewart's Army of Tennessee, Hardee's contingent when it arrived.

Tobacco now grows seasonally in some of the fields north of the Goldsboro Road where Hampton's cavalry engaged the Army of Georgia. (dd)

The beauty of the plan was that only Hoke's Division, astride and below the Goldsboro Road, would be visible to the advancing enemy. Stewart and Hardee would come crashing out of the woods and strike the unsuspecting Union advance on the Federal left flank.

To complete their deployment, Hampton volunteered Dibrell's cavalry division to erect temporary obstructions that would slow the Federal advance along the Goldsboro Road, allowing time for the Confederate infantry to arrive. The enemy would then be caught by the obliquely charging Southerners.

On the morning of March 19, the plan began to unfold. Leading Slocum's advance on the Goldsboro Road was the XIV Corps division commanded by Brig. Gen. William Carlin. "After marching about three miles [we] came up to our foragers who were skirmishing with the enemy," Carlin recalled. Hampton's troopers, as they had done the day before, were continuing to stubbornly contest the Yankee advance. The annoyed Carlin decided to send in one of his brigades, commanded by Col. Harrison Hobart, to drive off the Rebel cavalrymen.

Elements from Brig. Gen. James Morgan's XX Corps division advanced against Dibrell's cavalry in this field below the Goldsboro Road. (dd)

Hobart's Brigade pushed forward skirmishers and "charged the enemy, driving him from his works through the woods and undergrowth beyond and across a large field east of Cole's house . . . a distance of more than a mile. As soon as the front line gained the house . . . the enemy opened a heavy fire . . . the line immediately commenced constructing works in front of the house." As Hobart ground to a halt, Carlin's other brigades moved up and deployed on either side of his line.

Encountering stiff resistance around the Cole property, Carlin decided to send his men forward in a reconnaissance in force, to ascertain what exactly lay in front of them. Dibrell's men opened fire as Carlin's men approached. Also joining in the fight was Hampton's artillery. "All the guns . . . were admirably served," the South Carolinian wrote, "and their fire held the enemy in their front."

Advancing below the road, "the troops moved forward in good order," a Pennsylvania officer wrote, "through a dense thicket and swamp and charged again and again, with no chance of carrying the works in consequence of the impenetrable thicket and the depth of the swamp."

North of the road, Carlin ran into lead elements of the Army of Tennessee, who had arrived on the field and taken up Hampton's hand-picked position. The Federals encountered "a heavy line of the enemy," a Hoosier recalled. "[A] well-directed volley drove them back to their works, from behind which we received a terrific volley." The Confederate veterans ably repulsed the Yankee advance and kept their location hidden from their prying eyes.

With Carlin encountering stubborn resistance both

George Dibrell was a native of Tennessee and had served earlier in the war under Nathan Bedford Forrest. He would render invaluable service to Wade Hampton as he delayed the Union movement toward Goldsboro. After the war, Dibrell would serve ten years in the U.S. Congress. (loc)

Brig. Gen. William Carlin's division drove enemy cavalry across this ground north of the Goldsboro Road. (dd)

north and south of the road, his corps commander, Jefferson Davis, ordered up the division of Brig. Gen. James Morgan. Morgan deployed on Carlin's right. Reaching their assigned position, Morgan's men constructed "good log works."

As morning turned to afternoon, Hampton's preparations during the last few days were beginning to pay dividends. Carlin had been stopped not once, but twice. The time was ripe for the Confederates to throw a massive counter punch.

For Want of a Map

A simple, well-drawn map—something *so* simple that it can be easily overlooked. On the night of March 18, William Hardee, leading tired, foot-sore, hungry Confederates on the last leg of the march to Bentonville, was not aware of exact distances between his starting point near Elevation and the rendezvous designated by Johnston.

The Georgian was not to blame. As a whole, the Confederate high command was working with an inaccurate map of the surrounding area. Distances were off, sometimes by several miles.

That may not seem like much, but when dealing with a surprise assault, with multiple forces converging on one point, the distance of a few miles can be catastrophic. Mix in fatigue, battle-weariness—for Hardee's command, especially—and the lack of foodstuffs, and those extra miles could definitely mean the difference between victory and defeat.

Maps could make all the difference.

In 1862, Jedediah Hotchkiss drew an accurate map of the Shenandoah Valley for Thomas J. "Stonewall" Jackson, which proved invaluable for the Confederate general to outsmart his Union adversaries. Two years later, Hotchkiss was able to help Maj. Gen. John Gordon outline the Union dispositions prior to the climactic battle of Cedar Creek.

Conversely, in December of 1862, mismatching, inaccurate maps possessed by Army of the Potomac commander Maj. Gen. Ambrose Burnside and his Left Grand Division commander Maj. Gen. William Franklin led to the debacle at Fredericksburg.

Around Bentonville, Johnston tried to employ locals to help him navigate the road networks. Unfortunately, the help he received was not entirely accurate. Hardee's men did arrive in time for the battle, but they had to undertake a few extra strenuous miles to get there.

All because of the need of a simple map or mapmaker.

Standing near the North Carolina and Texas monuments at Bentonville is a smaller memorial to the men who fought in the Union armies during the battle. While the first Confederate monument appeared in 1895, it was not until the twenty-first century that the Federal monument was erected. Through the efforts of the North Carolina Department of the Sons of Union Veterans of the Civil War, the North Carolina Historical Commission approved that a monument to Union soldiers be placed on that battle in November 2011. A total of $10,000 was raised, and the monument was dedicated during the observance of the anniversary of Bentonville in 2013. Etched in the memorial are the insignia of the four Union corps that made up Sherman's armies, along with the names of the states the Federal soldiers hailed from. (dd)

Johnston's Grand Assault

CHAPTER SEVEN

MARCH 19, 1865—AFTERNOON/EVENING

Early in the morning, the Confederate infantry had taken their respective places behind the cavalry screen that Hampton had laid as cover. Hoke's Division filtered into their respective places southeast of the Upper Goldsboro Road, with their right flank resting near the thoroughfare. On the northwest side of the road, extending from the clearings around the Cole Plantation into the tall woods, were the North Carolina Junior Reserves. Their ranks were made up of 17- and 18-year-olds who had been recruited the previous year to help ease the manpower crisis in the Confederacy.

On the right of the young Tar Heels were the proud remnants of the Army of Tennessee. Alexander Stewart had taken up positions behind the Junior Reserves and their right flank, with horse artillery covering the gap between the Junior Reserves and the veteran soldiers.

Next came Stephen Dill Lee's command, under the charge of the fiery D. H. Hill. Hill extended the line further by latching onto Stewart's right flank. Lastly, a contingent from Benjamin Cheatham's corps, under Maj. Gen. William Bate, extended the Confederate line even further.

With the Army of Tennessee in line, Johnston could count on an approximate 10,000 muskets to carry out his flank attack.

After this deployment came the division of William Taliaferro, which was part of Hardee's command. Taking a position to the right of Bate, these men would have the unenviable task of trying to hold their alignment during the advance through a mature forest.

Lafayette McLaws' division arrived late in the morning. The Georgian stopped on the Goldsboro Road

The Army of Tennessee built these earthworks prior to its attack on the afternoon of March 19. The original log revetments remain. Visitors may get directions to reach this location from the staff at the Bentonville Battlefield Visitor Center. (dd)

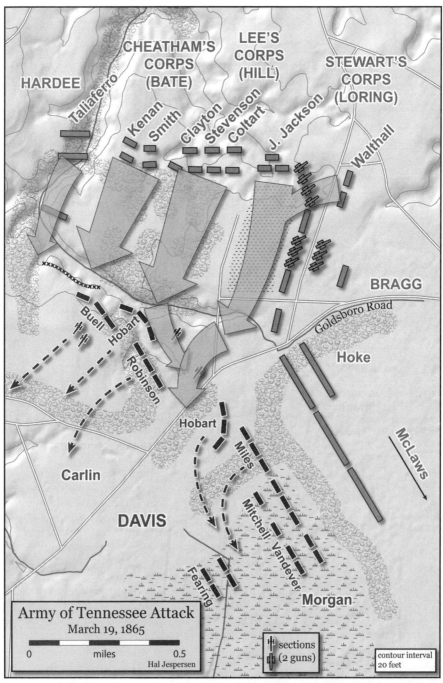

ARMY OF TENNESSEE ATTACK—Toward the middle of the afternoon of March 19, Johnston sent the Army of Tennessee forward in a massive assault. Despite the devastating losses suffered at Franklin and Nashville, the Confederate infantry performed extremely well. The Rebels swept away Brig. Gen. William Carlin's division before encountering stiff resistance from Brig. Gen. James Morgan's division.

and transferred to the extreme left of the Confederate line, extending out from Hoke's position.

Meanwhile, while Carlin's men withdrew from their earlier attack, a curious event was taking place behind the Union lines. "One of my officers brought to me an emaciated, sickly appearing young man . . . dressed in Confederate gray," Slocum remembered. "[H]e said he had been in the Union army, had been taken prisoner and while sick and in prison had been induced to enlist in the Confederate service. . . . [H]e said he had enlisted with the intention of deserting when a good opportunity presented itself."

The soldier went on to tell Slocum that he was from Syracuse, New York. As Slocum continued to question him, one of his staff officers rode up and recognized the man as an old acquaintance from Syracuse. This "galvanized Yankee" then revealed that a "very large force" was in front of Slocum, commanded by Joe Johnston.

A jolt shot through Henry Slocum. He was no longer facing Hampton's cavalry, but had a real fight on his hands against an enemy of undetermined number.

Slocum scribbled a note to an aide and ordered him to take it to Sherman, stating to "ride well to the right so as to keep clear of the enemy's left flank."

Until Sherman arrived with the Army of the Tennessee, Slocum would have to fight it out on his own.

As the fighting progressed through the day on March 19, Maj. Gen. Henry Slocum brought up troops to deploy in these woods and reinforce the Union line. (dd)

* * *

By early afternoon, Johnston was ready to launch his offensive. However, would his men show the same élan as they had done on numerous fields in the last three years? Or had their disasters in middle Tennessee and the long, bleak winter sapped that élan out of them?

At approximately 2:45 p.m., Hardee—who had been given command of the assault—urged the infantry out of their entrenchments and through the woods toward Carlin's infantry. One Tennessee soldier remembered his compatriots "advanced with a yell" and that "we could take the works or old Joe [Joseph Johnston] would not order it."

As the Army of Tennessee moved forward, one of the Junior Reserves said "it looked like a picture . . . several officers led the charge on horseback . . . with colors flying and line of battle in such perfect order." The pageantry of the advance was done "gallantly, but it was

Johnston launched his grand assault from this position. The Army of Tennessee marched across this field and engaged Brig. Gen. William Carlin's division, which was positioned in the woods on the far side of the field. (dd)

Gen. Braxton Bragg had a knack for snatching defeat from the jaws of victory. On March 19, he held true to form by withholding key Confederate troops, blunting the effectiveness of the main assault. (loc)

painful to see how close their battle flags were together." Their diminished numbers had tightened their ranks— "regiments being scarcely larger than companies and [a] division not much larger than a regiment should be."

They burst through the woods and into the fields. For one last time, with the same prowess they had unleashed on battlefields past, the soldiers let loose the "rebel yell."

The Confederate wave crashed into Carlin's division. "The enemy advanced heavy force on my front, right and left," Carlin said. "The attacks were repulsed . . . the men loading and firing coolly and deliberately, but the skirmish line on the left being forced back and the right of the line being turned, the remainder of the troops were compelled to give way."

An Indiana officer recalled that the enemy "came down on us. . . . A continuous fire . . . brought those in our front to a stand but, a heavy column striking both our flanks and turning them, we were compelled to withdraw."

As Carlin's men ran for their lives, the Rebels set their sights on Morgan's division below the Goldsboro Road. In an effort to slow the enemy advance, Jefferson Davis sent one of Morgan's brigades, under Brig. Gen. Benjamin Fearing, against the Confederates. A soldier in Fearing's brigade recalled that the Yankees met the Rebels "with volley after volley, mowing them down like grass." Still, the gray-clad soldiers kept coming, and Fearing's men broke before the onslaught.

South of the road, D. H. Hill's men now threatened to strike Morgan's rear. Morgan had already been contending with Hoke's Confederates to his front, and now he was about to be caught in a vice.

For unknown reasons, Hoke was held from the initial

assault. General Bragg had earlier in the day requested that McLaws reinforce Hoke. As a result, McLaws whiled away most of the day in an unnecessary position, withholding much-needed weight from Hardee's assault.

Hoke, at least, did get sent forward—although too late to be of optimal use to Hardee. When the North Carolinian's division stepped off, the men came on with a vengeance, rending the air with the "Rebel Yell" and slamming into Morgan's entrenchments, which had been built earlier in the day.

While elements of a Georgia brigade did succeed in making their way around the left flank of Brig. Gen. John Mitchell's brigade, most of Hoke's men were stymied at the Union breastworks by, as one soldier remembered, "the most terrific fire I ever listened to; nothing could withstand it." Hoke's assault stalled.

The fields of the Reddick Morris Farm, where the XX Corps repulsed the Rebel assaults following the collapse of Carlin's division. (pg)

But Federals quickly faced a new threat. "Our worst fears were soon realized by the enemy sweeping . . . on my immediate rear," an Illinois officer remembered. "My men immediately jumped to the other side of the works, receiving a withering fire as they did so. The enemy were quickly checked . . . by the rapid and effective fire that was poured into them. At this juncture the Fourteenth Michigan and Sixtieth Illinois charged them. . . ." Also participating in the counterattack was the 17th New York and the 10th Michigan. This counterpunch was enough to rock the Rebels back on their heels.

More help was on the way for the beleaguered Federal line in the form of Col. William Cogswell's brigade. Hurried up from the rear of the column, Cogswell's men "moved forward . . . through dense swamps . . . pressing back the enemy." This assault relieved the pressure on Morgan's men as the tired and disorganized Confederates withdrew back to the Goldsboro Road.

Even as Cogswell moved up to aid Morgan, Slocum continued to push more men to the front. They established a new line that stretched diagonally from the northwest to the southeast and across the Goldsboro Road. Supported by artillery, Slocum had a strong position from which to anchor the new Federal line that was sure to form once Sherman arrived.

Maj. Gen. Robert Hoke's division moved across this field to engage Brig. Gen. James Morgan's division. (dd)

Uncle Billy, in fact, was on his way. The couriers sent by Slocum had found Sherman, who soon learned that their comrades had "run up against Johnston's whole army." Sherman "sent back orders . . . to fight defensively" and that he would "come up with reinforcements." The Army of the Tennessee began its march to Slocum's aid "with the sound of cannon" echoing from Bentonville.

*   *   *

Throughout the day, the Confederates had shown they still possessed an awesome offensive prowess. Although his troops were reduced in numbers, Johnston's continued attacks struck hard and repeatedly. Arriving on the field to meet these assaults was Brig. Gen. Alpheus Williams' XX Corps. Slocum had ordered Williams to "bring forward with the least possible delay every regiment of his command." Much of that command would deploy on a farm owned by Reddick Morris, which would become the center of Slocum's reconstituted line.

Meeting them as they took up their new position was Taliaferro's division, consisting of the brigades of Brig. Gen. Stephen Elliott, Jr., and Col. William Butler. Screaming their old war cry, the gray coats "fell rapidly" as they advanced into the maelstrom and were then pushed back.

Still, the Confederates came on, even though the intensity of Union small arms and artillery ravaged the lines and the sandy soil, creating something akin to a mini sandstorm. Both brigades were ripped apart, which forced them to retreat back into the cover of the woods.

William Bate, whose division joined in the assaults on the Morris farm, recalled that his command "was in advance of our main battle line. . . . The enemy was in view. . . . He drove us back a short distance and formed a strong line, which our single line was too weak, from casualties and exhaustion, to successfully attack. The opposing lines being in easy rifle range, kept up a constant fire."

Ordered to move to the far right of the Confederate line, McLaws finally joined in the fray late in the afternoon. He remembered

the shells from the enemy bursting over the field we were in. My command was formed in two lines. . . . The enemy's fire became so troublesome that the troops were moved forward to the slope of the hill. . . . The sun was declining rapidly and the smoke settled heavy & dense over the country. . . . The firing was very rapid and continuous for some time after my brigades went forward, but gradually ceased as the darkness increased.

Although the bulk of McLaws' division would be engaged at the Morris farm, the experience of the South Carolina brigade under John Kennedy would be the most harrowing. Advancing just before dark, Kennedy struck Cogswell's brigade. During the assault, the pine needles in the woods around them caught on fire. The Palmetto Staters, veterans of Fredericksburg, Gettysburg, and the battles in the Shenandoah Valley, used the cover of the burning pines to mask their withdrawal back to more friendly confines.

This marker stands in the area where the Army of Tennessee crossed the Goldsboro Road to attack Morgan's division. (pg)

With the sun sinking below the western horizon, the firing began to dissipate. After a long day of fighting, Slocum would write admiringly that "the enemy had fought bravely." As both sides settled down for the night, the bravery exhibited by soldiers in blue and gray would be tested again when morning came.

Junior Reserves and Red Sashes

Fewer units underscored how dire the manpower situation in the South was than the Junior Reserves.

When the Confederate government passed the Conscription Act in 1862, the law stipulated that any man from the age of 18-35 was eligible for the draft, barring few exceptions. The law was later amended to include any male up to the age of 45.

Anyone younger or older was exempted from the Confederate service. However, if a male was—or could possibly pass for—17 years of age, he could be enlisted into the Junior Reserves until he turned 18, when he could then be sent to a combat unit.

In North Carolina, the Junior Reserves were originally organized into eight battalions and sent to non-combat zones to serve as guards, thus freeing other men to fight in front-line units. That was before the Confederacy began to run out of eligible men and, by late 1864, the rule was suspended. By 1865, these young men would stand in the firing line at Bentonville.

As you tour the Bentonville Battlefield, Stop 5 on the driving tour features interpretive panels that highlight the role of these young boys in the service of the Confederacy.

Another interesting conglomerate of units that served at Bentonville had, for most of the war, led a life of boredom protecting the ports of the Atlantic seaboard. This tedious service was punctuated by occasional run-ins with Union blockading vessels. The monotony ended with the fall of Wilmington in February 1865. During the retreat, these men had been collected by Lt. Col. John D. Taylor and were known as the "Red Infantry" because of their officer's red headgear and the trim that donned their artillery uniforms. Alongside a half-dozen companies of the 40th North Carolina Infantry—which would provide the nom de guerre of the entire unit—these displaced artillerymen would prove their prowess during Hoke's afternoon assaults by attacking earthen entrenchments instead of defending them.

OPPOSITE: A monument commemorating the battle of Bentonville was erected in 1927 by the North Carolina Historic Commission and the North Carolina Division United Daughters of the Confederacy.
(dd)

Reinforcements on the Road

CHAPTER EIGHT

MARCH 20, 1865

A rising sun that peeked through the pines on the morning of March 20 revealed the Army of the Tennessee marching toward the battlefield. After the frantic defense of his lines the day before, Henry Slocum no doubt would be happy to see them.

Leading the way was Col. Charles Catterson's brigade—part of Bvt. Maj. Gen. Charles Woods' division from the XV Corps. Not surprisingly, after reaching the upper Goldsboro Road east of the battlefield, Catterson's men ran into Rebel cavalry.

Interestingly, these Federals were being delayed by Confederate cavalry led by another face from the Army of Northern Virginia, Evander McIvor Law. Law had been a former infantry division commander. After receiving a wound at Cold Harbor, he requested to be relieved from command and left the army. Back in service after his recovery, Law was now fighting a slow withdrawal toward the left flank and rear of Johnston's line.

Encountering the gray troopers, Catterson employed a simple tactic to clear the road. The first regiment in column deployed as skirmishers and engaged the Confederates. When that regiment's ammunition ran low, Catterson called on the next regiment in line to take its place. This resulted in the Rebels being driven "briskly" back toward the main line.

"I found that the enemy was posted across the road behind high . . . works," an officer in the 46th Ohio recalled. "Believing that it could be carried by a rapid and spirited assault, I gave the command, 'double quick'

This view from the Morris farm looks out across the open fields where Johnston's assaults were repulsed on March 19. The Confederates attacked from the distance toward the cannon. (dd)

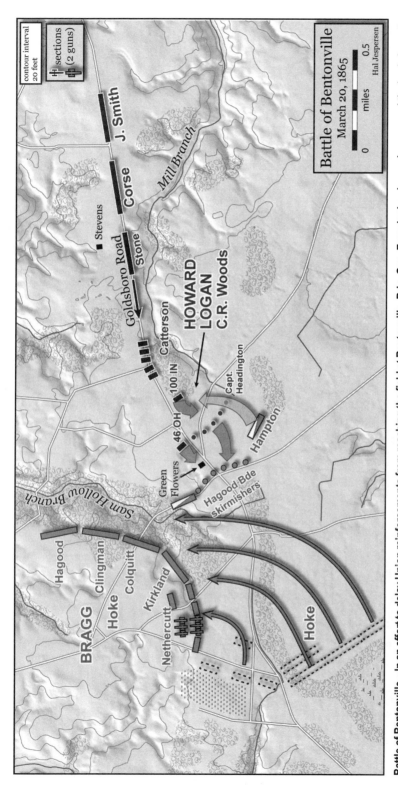

Battle of Bentonville—In an effort to delay Union reinforcements from reaching the field at Bentonville, Brig. Gen. Evander Law's cavalry engaged the lead elements of the Army of the Tennessee. The Confederate horsemen eventually gave way before superior numbers. To counter the arrival of this new Union force, Johnston swung his line back to face both to the east and west.

and the men took the step bravely and with cheers. . . . My men did not halt or check until they reached the works from which the enemy were flying in disorder and confusion."

Some of the Rebels, however, managed to launch a brief counterattack. "The Johnny cav[a]lry came dashing into our rear," remembered Theodore Upson of the 100th Indiana. "Generals Logan, Wood and others had followed our skirmish line closely. Col. Johnson saw the cav[a]lry coming out of the woods. He faced the Regiment towards them and the men fired a volley into them that scattered them, and his quick action no doubt saved not only us but the Generals from capture."

Brig. Gen. Evander Law's Confederate cavalry engaged and delayed the vanguard of the Army of the Tennessee on the morning of March 20. (loc)

* * *

Meanwhile, Johnston, apprised of the approach of the Army of the Tennessee, decided to pull Hoke back to a new position above the Goldsboro Road, swinging his left flank back to the north to meet the Yankees. Hoke had faced to the west on the first day of the battle; now he faced south and east, toward Howard's approaching wing. With the remnants of the Army of Tennessee facing Slocum, Hoke was free to establish this new line.

The veterans of Hoke's division soon began constructing earthworks in their new position. These entrenchments were buttressed with wood hewed by axes. The sound of the chopping attracted the attention of Union soldiers stationed immediately in front of Hoke's position, and a brief skirmish ensued.

Hoke's change of front did not go unnoticed by the Yankees. The 14th Michigan and 16th Illinois, both from Brig. Gen. William Vandever's brigade of Morgan's division, set out from their own position to locate the new enemy line. Captain J. W. Myers from the 14th wrote "light skirmishing commenced, and as I advanced increased rapidly until it extended along my entire line . . . the enemy

Hoke's division withdrew from this ground to a new position upon the approach of the Army of the Tennessee. (dd)

Union artillery on the Morris Farm engaged the enemy.
(NCDAH)

opened upon us with a battery of three guns, firing very rapidly and somewhat checking our advance. I ordered a halt and directed the men to cover themselves from the enemy's fire."

An Illinoisan recalled:

> [T]he ground was exceedingly swampy and covered with a dense growth of underbrush and vines. . . . Through this we rushed, without slackening our speed, for nearly half a mile, when we were met by a withering fire of musketry and by grape and canister. . . . When we received this fire the men were completely exhausted. . . . We fell back slowly and in better order than could have been expected under such circumstances.

Confederate fire, in part by the young men of the North Carolina Junior Reserves, brought the two regiments to a grinding halt.

Johnston was not the only one making dispositions through the morning hours. Slocum remembered, "Generals Baird and Geary, each with two brigades of their respective divisions . . . arrived on the field . . . Baird was moved out in front of our works beyond the advance position held by us on the preceding day." This infantry was a welcome sight to Slocum, but they were not the men he was expecting.

Although the division of Maj. Gen. William Hazen from the XV Corps had arrived, as the hour approached noon, Slocum was still left to wonder: where was the Army of the Tennessee?

"Smoked Yankees"

A wooden span over the Neuse River, Cox's Bridge, lay just north of the route the Army of the Tennessee would have to take to reach Bentonville. After a spirited engagement on the morning of March 20, Evander Law's Rebel cavalry withdrew to the bridge and set it ablaze, so as not to allow the Federals to use it as a crossing.

Four days later, however, the roles of Union and Confederate were reversed. Union troops encamped nearby were attacked by Southern cavalry. Among the Union forces encamped at Cox's Bridge was the 1st United States Colored Troops (USCT). Their chaplain, Henry Turner, remembered the works being manned by "smoked Yankees," which was what "the rebels call us." The fortified encampment was part of the makeshift defenses guarding Goldsboro.

Early on morning of March 24, the air was shattered by picket firing. The din of battle rose to a crescendo as the day wore on. A member of the 58th Indiana, the regiment responsible for maintaining the pontoon bridges across the river in the absence of the burned span, jotted in his diary that as the fighting grew in intensity, "the tattered banners were unfurled" and the "men stood ready for action."

Leaving the safety of the camp, the 1st USCT marched out and engaged in a sharp skirmish with elements of Wade Hampton's Confederate cavalry. One Union officer remembered that the Rebels "made a vigorous attack, opening some artillery upon our picket line. The attack was repulsed with small loss." Following the brief bombardment, the Rebel troopers finally withdrew.

Although minor in nature, the skirmish at Cox's Bridge underscored two important truths: the Confederates still possessed a fiery fighting spirit, and, second, as on other fields of battle, the USCTs proved their mettle against some of the best the Rebels had to offer in the form of Hampton's cavalry.

When the chaplain ventured back to where the USCT had traded volleys with the Confederate horse soldiers, he administered to the souls of five killed and nine wounded. The composure and battle-readiness of the USCT, who may have been referred to as "smoked Yankees" by their rebel counterparts, showed at Cox's Bridge that they could "smoke" the rebels in a different sense.

Sherman Arrives

CHAPTER NINE

MARCH 20, 1865—AFTERNOON/EVENING

Drowning out the sound of skirmish fire in the afternoon air was the tramping of the Army of the Tennessee. Marching along the Upper Goldsboro Road in the early afternoon, the divisions from Maj. Gen. John Logan's corps appeared on the field. Logan directed his subordinates, Brig. Gens. John Corse and John Smith, to deploy into a line of battle.

"We came to the immediate vicinity of the main line and went into position," recalled Maj. Thomas Osborn, Howard's Chief of Artillery, "as the troop came up and commenced operations to find the right of Slocum's line. We could guess where that was only by the geography of the country, its topography and what we could draw out of the citizens and the occasional sound of artillery [in] the neighborhood of Slocum's right."

As the afternoon wore on, Maj. Gen. Frank Blair's XVII Corps arrived. Blair posted Maj. Gen. Joseph Mower's division to the south, hoping to finally make contact with the Army of Georgia. The division of Brig. Gen. Giles Smith formed on Logan's right. Brigadier General Manning F. Force's division was held in reserve.

* * *

Skirmishers from the Army of the Tennessee moved through this area probing for the Confederate position upon their arrival on the battlefield. (dd)

In his official report, Joseph Johnston wrote one simple paragraph, indicating that "the enemy had three of his four corps present and well entrenched, the attack was not renewed." For the remainder of the day, his forces held their ground "in the hope that his greatly superior numbers might encourage him to attack, and to cover the removal of our wounded."

Johnston was hoping that he could induce Sherman to assault and bloody his army against his entrenched Confederates—similar to the assault at Kennesaw Mountain in Georgia in July 1864. His plan worked, he later wrote: "General Bragg's line was repeatedly attacked and the enemy repulsed, severely punished."

Johnston established his new position on March 20 beyond this tree line. (dd)

After the realignments of the morning had been completed, including the deployment of Lafayette McLaw's division to the Confederate left flank, Johnston could count approximately 20,000 men available for duty. His Southerners would be up against more than twice their number when the sun rose on March 21.

While Johnston shifted, so did Slocum, who moved his divisions up to occupy the ground that had been fought over on the 19th.

When Robert Hoke's division pulled back in the morning hours that day to better solidify the Confederate defensive line, there was one slight drawback to the North Carolinian's new position. By connecting with the Army of Tennessee, his line formed a salient—a bulge in the line—which was extremely vulnerable to an enemy attack from several sides. Luckily for the Confederates guarding this portion of the line, they had ample artillery support.

"Johnston's army occupied the form of a 'V,'" Sherman noted when he arrived on the battlefield, "the angle reaching the road leading from Averysboro [sic] to Goldsboro and the flanks resting on Mill Creek, his lines embracing the village of Bentonsville. General Slocum's wing faced one of these lines and General Howard's the other."

Federals immediately recognized the strength of the position. "They are . . . strongly entrenched and those who were on the Atlanta Campaign are much reminded of the way things used to be," wrote Maj. Henry Hitchcock, serving on Sherman's staff.

The ongoing Federal movement prompted what Hitchcock described as a "good deal of sharp skirmishing." This prompted many soldiers in blue to strengthen their new position. One Illinois officer from Blair's corps recalled that his regiment "threw up a light line of works in an open field facing a pine timber, and in the evening advanced into the wood and threw up a heavier line of works, keeping up a strong skirmish line in front."

Although the skirmishing was constant on March 20, the action never escalated to a full-scale engagement.

In the early afternoon, two regiments from Ohio and Missouri from Maj. Gen. William Hazen's division were ordered out to the skirmish line in an effort to make contact with Howard. In the process of moving past the vacated Confederate works—which Hoke had pulled back from earlier in the day—they advanced across a marshy area. When they popped out of the marsh, they provoked a response from North Carolinians under the command of Brig. Gen. William W. Kirkland.

Shortly afterwards, as Union forces attempted to establish a consistent skirmish line, the bold movements of the bluecoats attracted the veteran skirmishers of Hoke's Division. Iowans from Col. George Stone's brigade, who had been sent out to make contact with the Army of Georgia, provoked a response from the North Carolinians. Also joining the fight were the North Carolina Junior Reserves.

An Ohio officer remembered that his men "met the enemy pickets, driving them into their works." As good skirmishers are trained to do, though, the North Carolinians slowly backed toward their main line, moving up the slope on the other side of the marsh. Seeing the line on the crest of the slope, the Federals halted and began constructing works of their own.

Late in the evening, Howard finally made contact with skirmishers from Morgan's division. The threadbare link was enough. Sherman finally had his entire army group on hand to meet Johnston.

Finally reaching the battlefield, Maj. Gen. William Tecumseh Sherman established his headquarters in the field where this historical marker now stands. (pg)

XV Corps skirmishers in action on March 20. (NCDAH)

Although there was minimal pitched infantry fighting on the second day, Federal gunners received little rest. (NCDAH)

Uneasiness settled over the battlefield. "We spent the night where we had fought . . . with the dead all around us," wrote an Ohio soldier in the Army of Georgia. "Men prone upon their faces in death's deep abasement. . . . Here lies one, his head pillowed upon his folded arms, there one, his cheek pressed upon a stone as was Jacob's at Bethel. . . . We pass on where a lieutenant grasps a bush as if he died vainly feeling for a little hold upon earth and life."

With the coming dawn, many men would have to grasp a little tighter.

Salients

As Johnston's line evolved into the shape of a salient, it bore a striking resemblance to the position occupied by the Confederate Army of Northern Virginia during the battle of Spotsylvania Court House during the Overland Campaign in May 1864. Interestingly, what became known as the "Mule Shoe" at Spotsylvania and Johnston's Bentonville position were both formed because of the arrival of enemy forces on the battlefield and Confederate attempts to conform to the topography as a way to counter those arriving forces.

A salient is a section of a line that protrudes from the main line. Its natural bulge or wedge shape allows for an enemy to attack it from three sides: center, left, and right. Thus, the position negates the ability of defenders to concentrate their fire; instead, their fire diverges in those three separate directions. Making the formation even more precarious, the space within the salient is subject to enemy artillery fire from every direction.

At Spotsylvania, the Union Army of the Potomac successfully exploited the weakness of the "Mule Shoe." On two separate occasions, Federals launched attacks that punched holes in the Confederate lines. The second time resulted in the longest and most brutal hand-to-hand combat to take place during the American Civil War in an area aptly known afterwards as "the Bloody Angle."

Rather than withdrawing from the field, Johnston elected to stay. In doing so, he placed his army in a dire position.

A partial view of the ground occupied by Johnston's salient. (dd)

Harper House

Despite the carnage surrounding it, the Harper house survived the largest Civil War battle in North Carolina. (dd)

On the morning of March 19, XIV Corps Medical Director Waldo C. Daniels established his field hospital in the Reddick Morris house. As the day wore on, the Confederate assaults grew dangerously close to the hospital. For the safety of the wounded, Daniels decided to move the hospital a half-mile to the rear and occupy the John Harper house.

John Harper's family originally hailed from Harper's Ferry, Virginia, the sight of John Brown's Raid in 1859. Harper owned about 825 acres and built a two-story house there in 1855.

After moving the hospital to the Harper home, Daniels remembered that "about 500 men were brought in and operated on or dressed."

On March 21, wagons arrived at the house to pick up the wounded and transport them to Goldsboro. Daniels indicated that 700 soldiers were moved from the Harper house and its vicinity at the end of the battle.

John and Amy Harper (NCDAH)

A room in the first floor of the Harper house, as it may have looked as Surgeon Waldo Daniels oversaw the treatment of wounded soldiers. (dd)

The Armies Skirmish

CHAPTER TEN

MARCH 21, 1865

A scent of rain permeated through the pines and across the fields and marshes around Bentonville. Men stamped the ground to warm themselves, longing for a cup of coffee to ward off the chill, but the cold air penetrated their bones.

Uncle Billy's chief concern was reaching Goldsboro and resupplying his armies. Sherman admitted that "we had no object to accomplish by a battle." With Johnston's army still in his immediate front, though, Sherman would not be able to simply disengage and continue his march, lest the Confederates strike his marching columns and thus potentially repeat the events of March 19.

Meanwhile, the Confederates continued to improve their lines and fret over the Union intentions for March 21. In the very early hours of that Tuesday, reports filtered back from rebel scouts that Sherman would fight.

The prospect of a Union advance was further exacerbated by the erroneous report that came to Johnston's headquarters from one of his corps commanders, Lt. Gen. A. P. Stewart. The Tennessean reported an advance to the right of the line. The report proved to be unfounded—in truth, only a thin line of blue clad pickets were reshuffling their lines.

So, while Sherman saw "no object to accomplish" in initiating a battle that morning, Johnston was getting reports of Union offensive movements on his right flank. The real concern that morning, however, was on the opposite end of the Confederate line.

The vulnerable section of the Confederate line was the left flank, which was held primarily by the cavalry. Troopers under Law, Hampton, and Wheeler

Robert Hoke's division constructed these earthworks as part of Johnston's salient. (dd)

Skirmishers from Brig. Gen. Charles Woods' Union division moved across this field in the direction of the woods to engage the Hoke's division on March 21. (dd)

were all that stood between the enemy and the rear of Johnston's army.

In a microcosm that illustrated the depleted ranks of Johnston's army, it took all of the skeletal remnants of the units comprising McLaw's Division to fill the gap. D. August Dickert, a South Carolinian in John Kennedy's brigade, recalled they were "detached and placed on the left of Hoke; the cavalry deployed as skirmishers to our left. There was a considerable gap between our extreme left and the main body of cavalry." Dickert commanded "this break" "with a heavy hue of skirmishers." Even with Confederate infantry nearby, the Mill Creek Bridge and lifeline of Johnston's army was guarded by cavalry. This could portend disaster if a large Union force pressured this sector.

* * *

To keep up an aggressive front in the hopes that Johnston would be the one to retreat first, Sherman ordered Slocum and Howard "to press steadily with skirmishers alone, to use artillery pretty freely on the wooded space held by the enemy, and to feel pretty strongly the flanks of his position."

All along the Union lines, blue skirmishers pressed forward. A soldier in the Army of Georgia recalled that they "adopted the tactics of the Atlanta Campaign. . . . Our lines were pressed close to the enemy's works, compelling the Confederates to stand by their arms for fear of an assault." One Ohioan wrote, "we charged their picket line just in front of us."

One member of the North Carolina Junior Reserves recalled that the "almost continuous firing" that had been ongoing was starting to take a toll. He recorded

Looking out from the lines of the Army of the Tennessee toward Johnston's salient (dd)

that he barely slept a wink after being out on the picket line since the day before. Above the position held by the Junior Reserves, the commander of the 50th Illinois in the Army of the Tennessee wrote, "I sent Company C . . . to relieve a company of the Fifty-Seventh Illinois that was on the skirmish line to our front. About 10 a.m. I received orders to build a new line of works about 200 yards in my front."

As skirmishers plied their deadly trade, both sides dug deeper into the eastern North Carolina soil. The Confederates had cleared the area in front of their lines and placed abatis, sharpened tree branches set in a line facing toward the enemy. Some places even had logs running across the tops of the earthworks, called head logs, to protect the soldiers' head from sniper fire. What the Confederates lacked in numbers, they were eagerly trying to compensate for with their defensive measures— further proof that Johnston's forces intended to stay.

Through the course of the action, a group of Georgians sallied out of their lines and set fire to the Cole home, which sat on the ground that had played so prominently in the early stages of the battle. After removing the Cole structures from "further use by Yankee sharpshooters," the opposing sides settled down to taking random potshots from the skirmish line at each other.

Throughout the morning, a "steady rain prevailed,"

Sherman wrote—showing the casualness of the Union army commander's plans for the day. Perhaps it was the weather, Sherman's orders, or the mood at headquarters that caused Henry Hitchcock to write, "I do not suppose there will be a heavy assault made by us in front."

He could not have been more wrong, for over on the Union right, one of Sherman's most aggressive commanders was about to turn the battlefield situation upside down.

The Henry Rifle

The Civil War illustrated the wonders of technology in mid-nineteenth century America. Railroads and the telegraph were used by the military of both sides. Perhaps the most technological advancement for the army, however, was in the use of weaponry with the emergence of repeating firearms. One of the most famous rifles to emerge from the conflict was the Henry Rifle.

Designed by Benjamin Tyler Henry, the rifle that bore his name was manufactured by Oliver Winchester at the New Haven Arms Company in New Haven, Connecticut. On July 1, 1862, the rifle was made available for sale to the public. Produced with both brass and iron frames, the weapon was loaded by inserting .44 cartridges into a tube located below the barrel. The tube could hold 16 rounds. A soldier then pushed forward a lever near the trigger guard, which simultaneously cocked the weapon and pushed a fresh round into the chamber. The gun was then ready to fire.

Although Federal units in the Eastern Theater would be armed with the Henry, it was predominately used by men in the Army of the Tennessee and the Army of the Cumberland. At Bentonville, three of Sherman's infantry regiments carried the Henry: the 7th Illinois, 64th Illinois, and 66th Illinois.

The 7th would skirmish with Law's cavalry as the Army of the Tennessee approached the battlefield on March 20. The 64th played an important role in the fighting on March 21. Probably the most famous of these regiments, though, was the 66th. Known as Birge's Western Sharpshooters, this regiment was originally constituted as the 14th Missouri at the beginning of the war before being renamed the 66th Illinois in the fall of 1862. Interestingly, the regiment was also made up of men that hailed from Ohio, Wisconsin, and

A Henry rifle hangs on display in the Bentonville Battlefield Visitor Center. (dd)

Minnesota. Similar to the 1st and 2nd United States Sharpshooters that served in the Army of the Potomac, these Westerners specialized in skirmish fighting and sniping. Along with the battle of Bentonville, the regiment could count Fort Donelson, Shiloh, Corinth, and Atlanta among its honors.

Today, one can view a Henry Rifle in the Bentonville Battlefield museum.

Reconnaissance in Force

CHAPTER ELEVEN

MARCH 21, 1865—AFTERNOON/EVENING

Just as Federal reinforcements had arrived the day before, Johnston would receive his on March 21. The Confederates were augmented by Maj. Gen. Frank Cheatham's 1,000-man contingent of the Army of Tennessee. Reaching the field that morning, the men were excited at the opportunity to fight under the popular Joseph Johnston, but the march to the field of battle had been arduous and tiring. Cheatham had driven his men more than 25 miles through the night to reach the battlefield.

As Cheatham's veterans rested, a nightmare was starting to occur on the Confederate left flank. Evander Law was anxiously reporting a dire situation to Wade Hampton.

As Sherman's soldiers probed the Confederate line that morning, Maj. Gen. Joseph Mower, commanding a division in Blair's XVII Corps, received orders to extend the Union right flank. A hard charger, Mower was a veteran of Corinth and the Vicksburg and Red River campaigns. When Mower reached his new position, Blair gave him permission to launch a reconnaissance in force.

"Learning that a road leading from the right of the line crossed Mill Creek by a ford, I pushed my command down that road for the purpose of closing in on the enemy's flank," Mower later explained. Encountering a swamp, he found "it necessary to halt the Third Brigade some three quarters of an hour to allow the First Brigade to pass the swamp."

From the other side of the swamp, Law's pickets

The Texas Monument at Bentonville. One of the more famous Texas units, the 8th Texas Cavalry, played a critical role in driving back Maj. Gen. Joseph Mower's assault on the last day of the battle. (dd)

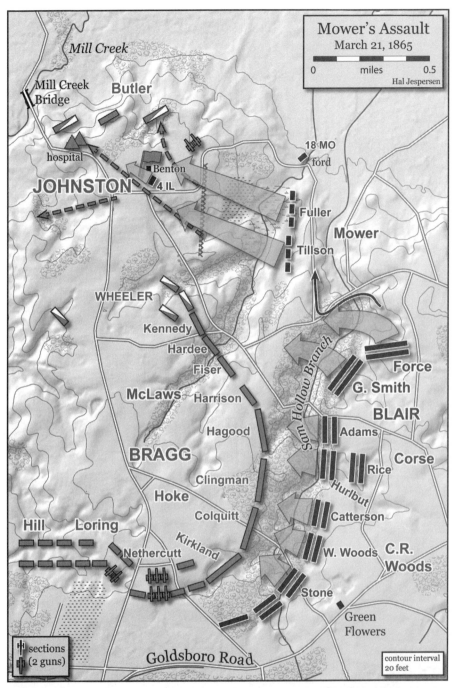

MOWER'S ASSAULT—Late on the morning of March 21, Brig. Gen. Joseph Mower launched a reconnaissance in force toward the Confederate left. The Yankees quickly overran the thin enemy line and came dangerously close to cutting Johnston's line of retreat across Mill Creek. Recognizing the threat, the Rebels quickly counterattacked, forced Mower to withdraw, and secured their position.

spotted Mower's division coming into position directly in front of the skirmish line. This large concentration of the enemy across from the already-thin Confederate left unsettled Law.

Hampton instructed Law to ask Maj. Gen. Joseph Wheeler to extend his line in support. Wheeler was also spread thin and did not have the men available to meet the request.

The situation was grim. Like a blue tidal wave, these veteran Union soldiers were advancing on the precarious Confederate forces tasked with guarding the critical left flank.

Mower's division moved across this ground to assault the Confederate line in the distance. (dd)

"As we emerged into an open field one of General Mower's staff brought an order to 'double quick,'" recalled Brig. Gen. John Fuller, commanding one of Mower's brigades:

> *This was immediately repeated, and the whole line passed over the field at this step. About this time the enemy used some artillery against us, and as we reached the opposite woods the major-general ordered a halt. This was repeated by my staff . . . along a portion of the line . . . but the men, who had caught sight of an abandoned caisson, were cheering so as to render it impossible to hear the orders, and continued to run forward till they reached the enemy's intrenched line, from which he ran at full speed.*

Mower had encountered and quickly driven away Evander Law's cavalrymen. The momentum gained by this quick victory inspired the Yankees forward.

"The major-general rode to the front of my brigade," Fuller continued, "and in person ordered the line again to advance, whereupon we passed over the enemy's [e]ntrenchments and occupied the crest of the hill beyond."

Streaming forward, Mower's Federals had broken through Johnston's line and had reached the eastern outskirts of Bentonville. Unbeknownst to Mower, beyond the village, just to the west, lay the Mill Creek bridge and Johnston's only line of retreat. But at this critical moment in the battle—and perhaps for the Confederacy—Mower was informed that his left did not link with the rest of the

If Mower's infantry reached the Mill Creek bridge, they would effectively cut off Johnston's only line of retreat from the battlefield. (cm)

Union line. "I ordered him back to connect with his own corps," Sherman later explained.

Pursuant to orders, Mower attempted to shift his men to the south. This moment of hesitation was enough to allow the Rebels to counterattack.

With his headquarters overrun, Johnston sent out instructions to Cheatham's newly arrived command to send in reinforcements to drive back Mower. A recipient of these orders was a brigade commanded by Col. Robert Anderson. A staff officer rode with Anderson to point out his brigade's new position.

Also encamped in rear of the now-demolished Confederate left flank was a cavalry brigade led by Col. Baxter Smith. Comprised of Arkansas, Tennessee, and Texas cavalrymen, these troopers had a reputation for being tenacious fighters. Among their number was the 8th Texas Cavalry. Known as "Terry's Texas Rangers," after their first commander, Benjamin Franklin Terry, these men were veterans of Shiloh, Perryville, Stones River, and Chickamauga. Although small in number, these men would loom large in the coming minutes.

The Confederates launched desperate counterattacks across this field in an effort to stabilize their broken left flank. (dd)

As Smith's cavalry arrived on the field and prepared to counterattack, "the skirmishers of the enemy . . . were retiring, and also drawing off toward their left and our right . . ." Anderson wrote. "I at once changed front so as to correspond with this movement of the enemy. After proceeding a short distance in the new direction, the Eighth Texas Cavalry came up on my right and charged in conjunction with me."

"Forward Rangers!" went the battle cry. Although more than Texas were represented, the order fit.

From rifles and carbines, the initial Rebel volley bellowed forth. With their weapons emptied, the cavalrymen then resorted to their weapon of choice in close combat: revolvers.

Mower's ranks staggered as the situation began to turn. "The result of the charge was more than could have properly been expected from troops so suddenly called upon to charge so superior a force," recounted Joe Wheeler, watching from nearby.

Joining in the assault was the rest of Frank Cheatham's division, with Cheatham himself leading the way.

Dismounted Confederate cavalry under Lt. Col. James Lewis and Col. D. G. White also lent their firepower to the attack. This hodgepodge force "threw the enemy in a most rapid and disorderly retreat."

Colonel John Tillson, commanding Mower's other brigade, wrote that "the enemy charged in two

These remaining buildings are some of the few that once made up the vibrant village of Bentonville. (cm)

battalion lines, striking the left almost perpendicularly and extending to the center. . . . My left thus flanked was compelled to slowly give ground." A soldier from the 32nd Wisconsin remembered, "the Johnnies . . . came down in overwhelming numbers. . . . Then was a critical moment for us, our flank was turned and the Johnnies were all around us." The Badger proudly recalled that "the 32nd was not whipped, she stood her ground and never fell back one foot until ordered."

Pressed from three sides, Mower ordered his men to withdraw and rejoin the main line.

Realizing afterwards the opportunity that Mower's offensive had presented in cutting off the Confederate line of retreat, Sherman lamented the order to halt the attack. "I think I made a mistake there," he later admitted, after hindsight had given him a better view of the battle, "and should rapidly have followed . . . with the whole of the right wing which . . . could not have resulted otherwise than successfully to us."

After a harrowing afternoon, the Confederate line was finally reestablished. "With the assistance of some

infantry, we filled all the space between the left of our
[e]ntrenched line and Mill Creek, thus securing our
communication from further menace from any force,"
Wheeler remembered.

The events of the day, however, were not lost on Joe
Johnston. His lines were too thin. It was clear that he had
overstayed his time at Bentonville. Late that afternoon,
Johnston began making plans to abandon the field.

Before the calendar turned, Johnston would begin
his withdrawal. With a cold rain falling, the Rebels
withdrew from their breastworks. The Confederates
were leaving Bentonville behind.

"Sherman's course cannot be hindered by the small
force I have," Johnson lamented. "I can do no more to
annoy him."

The Death of a Son

In a war that had claimed hundreds of thousands
of sons, the closing hours of Bentonville saw another
promising, energetic young Southerner's life cut short in
particularly poignant fashion.

During the early afternoon of March 21, 16-year-
old Willie Hardee rode into the bivouac of the 8th Texas
Cavalry. Willie was the son of Lt. Gen. William Joseph
Hardee, and he hoped to find some action at Bentonville.
He hoped to find it with the Texans, whose reputation as
hard-fighters offered much allure.

Willie had already seen some action serving with
his father in parts of the Atlanta campaign the previous
summer. Earlier in 1865, Willie had left school in Georgia
to join an artillery unit, but found life as a cannoneer dull
and unsatisfying. By March, the elder Hardee had tried
to stash his only son on his personal staff in order to keep
him as safe as possible on the battlefield, but this did not
satisfy the young ambitious boy, who yearned to earn his
rank alongside his accomplished father.

Willie and his new comrades in the 8th Texas were
soon called into action when Mower's attack rolled
through Johnston's headquarters and threatened to shear
the Confederate left from their only avenue of escape.
The Confederates needed to save the bridge that was
the lifeline of the Army of the South. As the 8th Texas
and the 4th Tennessee Cavalry came into line under the
supervision of Hardee, the lieutenant general noticed a

familiar face in the battle line. Doffing his cap, Hardee acknowledged the presence of his son.

The impetuous charge caught the advancing Union skirmishers by surprise, and a lively firefight ensued. Slamming into the enemy skirmishers, the cavalry drove back Mower's division.

Hardee, euphoric in the aftermath of the successful assault, turned to Wade Hampton. "This was nip and tuck," Hardee said, "and for a time I thought Tuck had it."

"Tuck" might not have had it, but Hardee had not seen the end of it. During the melee through the woods, a Union bullet had slammed into Willie, who was held on horseback by a Texan comrade. As his father looked on, the younger Hardee was gingerly placed on a stretcher and carried to the rear, where a waiting ambulance removed the teenager to Hillsborough, North Carolina.

There under the tender care of his mother and sister, surrounded by extended family, Willie Hardee lingered for another two days. On March 23, 1865, he breathed his last. Willie had gone to war looking for action and adventure. Instead, he died under his father's command during in the last throes of the dying Confederacy.

OPPOSITE: A lone rose lies next to the headstone of Willie Hardee in the cemetery of St. Matthews Episcopal Church in Hillsborough, North Carolina. (dd)

The Battle Ends

CHAPTER TWELVE

LATE MARCH

Late on the night of March 21 and into the early morning hours of the next day, Johnston abandoned the battlefield to Sherman. Although Confederates relinquished the field to the enemy, the engagement had a more positive outcome for them than a defeat should have suggested.

Bentonville, if only fleetingly, showed the military prowess that still burned in the chest of the proud ragtag collection of soldiers that now comprised the Army of the South. The assault of March 19 best exemplified that. Their dogged determination, however, to remain on the defensive the next two days could have resulted easily in an unmitigated and complete disaster for the Confederates.

Johnston would write to Lee that "the spirit of the army is greatly improved." Unfortunately, that "spirit" which the Virginian also rated as "excellent" could not compensate for the large disparity in numbers on the battlefield.

Four days after Bentonville, Lee would launch his last offensive around Richmond and Petersburg by attacking a Federal fortification called Fort Stedman. But there, too, the problem of manpower crippled the Confederacy.

While Bentonville may have raised the spirits of some in the ranks, time was quickly closing in on the withering Confederate armies.

Ironically, credit for the relative Confederate success at Bentonville can go to a man who had been sent home the previous summer in defeat. Johnston's assignment,

The Goldsboro Rifles monument at Bentonville guards the entrance to the Confederate cemetery. In the surrounding fields, Wade Hampton's cavalry delayed the advance of the Army of Georgia during the opening stages of the battle. (dd)

Similar to the marble and granite monuments nearby, the Harper house stands today as memorial to the men who were treated there from both armies. (dd)

when he had been placed back in command, was to stop Sherman's advance. Realizing the impossibility of that, he decided to strike an isolated wing of the Union army. Surprisingly enough, Johnston's plan nearly succeeded. Aided by the redoubtable Wade Hampton and William Hardee, the grand assault on the first day stampeded an entire Union division and came very close to driving from the field another. A lack of aggressiveness on the part of Braxton Bragg to press home the assault allowed Henry Slocum's units to hold the field and eventually consolidate their lines and await reinforcements.

For William Tecumseh Sherman, the battle at Bentonville and the engagement at Averasboro were fights he did not want. His main concern was reaching Goldsboro to resupply his armies—which Sherman eventually did on March 23. Food, rather than fighting, was foremost in his mind. This concern perhaps contributed to Sherman's complacency when he heard, after Averasboro, that a major Confederate force was operating in the same area he was attempting to march through. Recognizing that his men had to be fed, and that his three-day stay in the Bentonville vicinity had stripped the area of supplies, may have contributed to Sherman's reluctance not to press home Mower's assault.

Bentonville would quickly be overshadowed by the euphoria that erupted with the Confederate surrenders that ended the American Civil War. But for three days in March, the battle showed the determination, sense of pride and valor, and spirit that still emanated from the Confederate army.

The devastation wrought by the battle forced John Harper to become a sharecropper after the war. Today, he rests in a cemetery adjacent to the graves of Confederate soldiers who were treated in his home. (dd)

A Union soldier, walking over the contested ground, summed up the action at Bentonville—and the last measure of the principle Confederate force in the Western Theater. "I was amused at one tree, through which seven cannon balls had passed, yet it continued to stand," he said. "That tree must have been a rebel."

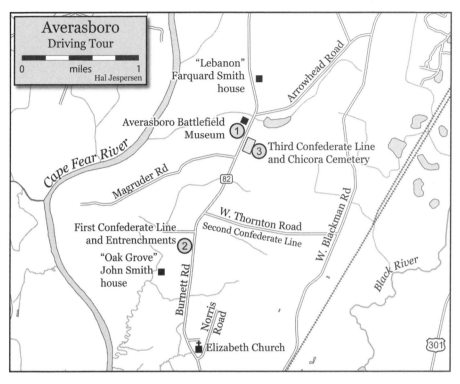

$\mathcal{A}\textit{verasboro}$

DRIVING TOUR #1

TOUR STOP 1: Averasboro Battlefield Museum

3300 North Carolina 82 Dunn, NC 28334
GPS: N 35.26620 W 78.67225

The tour for the Averasboro battlefield begins at the Averasboro Battlefield Museum. There is no admission fee to the museum; however, hours vary. Be sure to check www.averasboro.com/FAQs for operating hours. Inside, you may view exhibits relating to the battle.

(pg)

➡ TO TOUR STOP 2

Proceed out of the museum parking lot and make a right onto North Carolina Route 82. Proceed 1.6 miles west. You will see the Civil War Trails signs on the right and a small turnoff. Confederate entrenchments are still present.

N 35.15128 W 78.40389

TOUR STOP 2: First Confederate Line and Entrenchments

You are now standing along the first Confederate line, occupied by Col. Alfred Rhett's brigade from Brig. Gen. William Taliaferro. The day before the battle, Rhett was captured by Union cavalry and command devolved to Col. William Butler.

(dd)

The William Smith house (dd)

As the battle progressed on the morning of March 16, Union soldiers attacked this position, advancing toward you through the open fields to your immediate front. Encountering stiff resistance, Maj. Gen. Henry Slocum ordered a brigade of Ohio and Illinois units under Col. Henry Case to flank this position. Case advanced toward this position from the tree line to your right. This maneuver made the position untenable, and the Rebels withdrew to their second line, just to the north. A monument to the men of the XX Corps who fought and died during the battle stands at the far end of the earthworks.

Following the collapse of the first Confederate line, the XX Corps divisions under Brig. Gens. William Ward and Nathaniel Jackson continued their advance toward the second Confederate line. This position was manned by Col. Stephen Elliot's brigade, also from Taliaferro's division. Despite being reinforced by the 1st Georgia Regulars, the 32nd Georgia, and the 2nd South Carolina, Elliot was overwhelmed by a sheer force of numbers.

While a historical marker notes the Second Confederate Line, unfortunately, no wayside exists. You can, however, view the location of this line while standing at the entrance to the First Confederate line. The line of pine trees to your left along West Thornton Road traces the position.

To your immediate left front is "Oak Grove," the home of the John Smith family. The Smiths were prominent landowners in the area. During the battle, Smith and his wife, along with five of their children, left the house lest they be caught up in the fighting. Later, the house was used as a field hospital. The house originally stood across the road from its present location, in the vicinity of the private residence to your immediate front.

South of Oak Grove is the William Smith House. As Union soldiers marched past the home toward the First Confederate Line, Smith's widow, Mary, and her children remained inside. After the fighting had subsided, the Federals used the dwelling as a field hospital, with many of the dead being buried nearby.

Oak Grove and the Smith House are both private property; please respect the owners' rights.

Oak Grove (dd)

Lebanon, located on the Averasboro battlefield just north of the third Confederate line, was the home of Farquhard and Sarah Smith. Here, the Confederates established a field hospital. After the battle, one of the Smith daughters, Janie, wrote, "It makes me shudder when I think of the awful sights I witnessed." Despite being a hospital, Maj. Gen. Joseph Wheeler took tea with the Smiths. Today, the house is private property—please respect owner's rights. (dd)

TO TOUR STOP 3

Make a left out of the parking area. Proceed 0.9 miles east on North Carolina Route 82. As you drive, you will notice a sign for the Confederate Second Defensive Line. There is no safe parking or turn off, so please proceed until you reach the parking lot for the Confederate Third Defensive Line and Chicora Cemetery, on the right.

N 35.158 W 78.40372

BATTLE OF AVERASBORO
Phase Two - March 16, 1865

You are standing at the center of the second phase of fighting in the Battle of Averasboro, March 15, 16, 1865.

On the morning of March 16th, after the fight of the preceding afternoon around John Smith's house 2 miles south on this road, Union General H. J. Kilpatrick's cavalry found a back road (A) circled to the rear of the Confederate position (E-2). The Union cavalry (B) attempted to use this road to flank the Confederates, but was stopped by Colonel G. P. Harrison's brigade of McLaw's division (C) after moving only a short distance.

General W. B. Taliaferro decided to abandon the Confederate second position (E-2) after finding his men in danger of being flanked. At 1:00 P.M. he withdrew to the third and final line of earthworks (E-3), where he was assisted by McLaw's division on his left and Wheeler's dismounted cavalry on his right. Rhett's disorganized brigade (D) was held in general reserve behind the junction of this road (E) and the Smithfield road (F).

The Union forces soon advanced and established a strong line (G) immediately in front of the Confederate third line. From this new position they pressed the Confederates all afternoon and part of the evening, but were unable to break the line. At 8:00 P.M. General W. J. Hardee, commanding the Confederate forces at Averasboro, having accomplished his objectives, began withdrawing his corps along the Smithfield road. Wheeler's cavalry was left behind to cover the retreat. By 4:00 A.M. on March 17th, all Confederate units had

been withdrawn leaving the Union forces in control.

General Hardee wished to accomplish two things by contesting the Union advance at Averasboro. The first objective was to determine for General Joseph E. Johnston, commander of all Confederate forces in the Carolinas, whether Sherman's army was advancing on Raleigh or Goldsboro. The Confederates learned it was moving on Goldsboro. The second objective was to stretch out the distance between Sherman's left and right wings (which were moving on parallel roads) in order to give General Johnston a chance to concentrate his smaller army and destroy the Union left wing before the right wing could come to its assistance. Both of these objectives were fully accomplished. The stage was now set for the greater Battle of Bentonville, fought 23 miles east on March 19-21, 1865.

NOTE.
In order to better understand the battle it is best to read the large map marker "Phase One" which is located two miles south on this road.

TOUR STOP 3: Third Confederate Line and Chicora Cemetery

Major General Lafayette McLaws' division held the third, and final, Confederate line. Rain and exhaustion helped to slow the Union advance against McLaws. Arriving on the field to assist their XX Corps comrades was the XIV Corps division under Brig. Gen. James Morgan. Since Case's flanking attack had worked so well earlier

in the day, Morgan decided to send Brig. Gen. William Vandever's brigade to attack McLaws' right. Fortunately, Confederate cavalry under Maj. Gen. Joseph Wheeler arrived on the field to block Vandever's advance. Darkness finally brought an end to the fighting.

The remains of 56 Confederate soldiers who died at Averasboro rest in Chicora Cemetery. Deriving its name from the Native American word for "Carolina," the cemetery was established shortly after the battle. On May 10, 1872, the Smithville Memorial Association dedicated

TOP: The entrance to Chicora Cemetery (pg)
ABOVE: The United Daughters of the Confederacy erected a memorial in memory to those who rest there. (dd)

a monument to the dead. In 1904, the association became the Chicora Chapter of the United Daughters of the Confederacy.

In the cemetery stand memorials to Confederate soldiers from North Carolina (left), McLaws' division (center), and South Carolina (right) killed in battle. (dd)

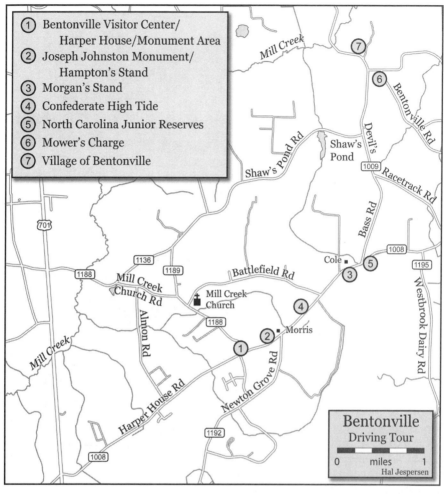

1. Bentonville Visitor Center/
   Harper House/Monument Area
2. Joseph Johnston Monument/
   Hampton's Stand
3. Morgan's Stand
4. Confederate High Tide
5. North Carolina Junior Reserves
6. Mower's Charge
7. Village of Bentonville

Bentonville
Driving Tour

0   miles   1

Hal Jespersen

(dd)

DRIVING TOUR #2

TOUR STOP 1: Bentonville Visitor Center
Harper House/Monument Area

5466 Harper House Road
Four Oaks, NC 27524
N 35.30598
W 78.32491

(dd)

The battlefield tour for Bentonville begins at the Bentonville Visitor Center. Inside, you will find a museum with exhibits and a short film that places the battle in the overall context of the Civil War. Hours vary, so be sure to check http://www.nchistoricsites.org/bentonvi/ for operating hours.

Tours are offered of the nearby Harper house. As the battle raged, John Harper; his wife, Amy; and six children (they had nine altogether) sought safety on the second floor of the building. Its close proximity to the battlefield made the house a natural location for a field hospital. The Harpers would care for men from both sides during and after the fighting.

Interestingly, the two outbuildings are not original to the site. They were moved to the location when the state of North Carolina acquired the property in 1957.

In the field adjacent to the Harper House, you will notice a solitary marker surrounded by a small split rail fence. This is not a monument to the battle; it is the grave of Sam Thornton, one of the subsequent owners of the Harper House. Thornton operated a general store located in the vicinity of the modern Visitor Center. You may view a photograph of Mr. Thornton in one of the displays inside.

Across from the Visitor Center you will find monuments commemorating the service of soldiers from North Carolina and Texas. There is also a monument for

(dd)

Sherman's armies. While the Texas monument was dedicated in 1964, both the North Carolina Monument and the Federal monument are relatively new to the site. The United Daughters of the Confederacy-Harper House Bentonville Chapter dedicated the North Carolina monument in 1992. In March 2013, to commemorate the 148th Anniversary of the battle, the Sons of Union Veterans erected the monument for the Federal soldiers who fought at Bentonville.

Nearby is the Harper family cemetery. It is shared with another family that owned the property after the war, the Dunns. Members of the Dunn family still reside in the area. Along with the Harper cemetery is a Confederate cemetery. Some of the Confederate wounded who were cared for in the Harper house rest there. While some of the graves are marked, many of these soldiers lay in a mass grave between the split-rail fences.

⟶ TO TOUR STOP 2

Make a right out of the parking lot for the visitor center. At the intersection turn left. Proceed two-tenths of a mile and turn left into the parking lot. You will see a small parking lot and a statue to Joseph Johnston. You are now in the area of Lieutenant General Wade Hampton's stand on March 19.

N 35.30639 W 78.31933

(dd) (pg)

TOUR STOP 2: Joseph Johnston Monument/Hampton's Stand

Through this area on the morning of March 19, Lt. Gen. Wade Hampton's cavalry delayed the advance of the XIV Corps. Hampton's troopers were deployed on both sides of the road and faced in the direction of the Visitor Center. To assist them in their fight, the troopers constructed makeshift barricades. Engaging the Federals, Hampton's men steadily withdrew toward the Willis Cole farm.

Normally, Union cavalry would be leading an infantry column. Kilpatrick's inability to punch through the Confederate screen at Aversaboro, however, infuriated Sherman. The horsemen were placed farther back in the marching order, forcing the Federals to use infantry to clear the road of Hampton's troopers—a role they were not accustomed to.

The Johnston monument rests on a battlefield that Johnston himself abandoned to the enemy after three days of fighting. The bronze statue is relatively new, having been dedicated in March 2010. The parcel is actually on private property and is maintained by the Sons of Confederate Veterans.

➤ TO TOUR STOP 3

Turn left out of the parking lot, proceed approximately one mile and you will see a sign on your right labeled "Morgan's Stand Tour Stop." Make a right into the loop and a wayside will explain the action that happened here.

N 35.18878 W 78.17998

TOUR STOP 3: Morgan's Stand

In the open field north of the Harper House Road stood home of Willis Cole. His plantation would form nucleus of the first day's battle. In the open fields beyond the house site, the Army of Tennessee engaged and smashed Brig. Gen. William Carlin's division of the XIV Corps. Continuing their drive south of the road and into the fields directly behind you, the Confederate infantry sliced into the rear of Brig. Gen. James Morgan's division. Morgan's soldiers had been engaged with Maj. Gen. Robert Hoke's division when they were forced to turn and meet this new threat. Regiments from Illinois, Michigan, and New York immediately faced about and counterattacked. This assault, along with arriving Union reinforcements, helped push the Rebels back and stabilize Morgan's line. Morgan's stand south of the road was crucial in halting the Confederate line and preventing further damage to the Army of Georgia.

➤ **TO TOUR STOP 4**

For the next stop, you will back track approximately one-half mile and the stop will be to your right. A sign on your right will read "Confederate High Tide Tour Stop." Pull in to the turn-off and you are at the nadir of the Confederate advance on March 19.

N 35.18502 W 78.18565

TOUR STOP 4: Confederate High Tide

You are now standing on the Reddick Morris farm. Carlin's division streamed to the rear and Morgan engaged the Rebels, Maj. Gen. Henry Slocum rushed up men from the XX Corps and established a new line here. Through middle of the afternoon into the evening, Johnston's Confederates launched several different assaults in an effort to dislodge the Yankees. The Federals, however, had an advantage in numbers and artillery. The Confederate attacks were turned back in quick succession. After failing to carry the Morris farm, Johnston's forces withdrew at nightfall to their original line.

➤ **TO TOUR STOP 5**

Make a left out of the turn-off and proceed down Harper House Road, approximately one-mile. At the corner of Harper House Road and Bass Road, you will see a sign "N.C Junior Reserves Tour Stop." Please use caution as there is not a substantial turn off in this area.

N 35.18971 W 78.17844

TOUR STOP 5: North Carolina Junior Reserves

The North Carolina Junior Reserves, part of Robert Hoke's division, held this position during the first two days of the battle. During the Confederate assault on March 19, the Junior Reserves remained here and not participate in the attack the fighting to the south against Morgan's division. On March 20, with the approach of the Army of the Tennessee from the east, Johnston contorted his line into the shape of an inverted V, forming a dangerously vulnerable salient in the process. Confederate infantry on this part of the line, including the Junior Reserves, withdrew to Johnston's new position to the north. During this maneuver, the Junior Reserves successfully engaged and pushed back enemy skirmishers throughout the surrounding area.

➤ TO TOUR STOP 6

Proceed down Bass Road, away from Harper House Road. At one-half mile continue onto Devil's Racetrack Road. In another approximate half-mile turn right onto Westbrook Lowgrounds Road (County Route 1189). At the intersection to your right, of County Route 1189 and Betonville Road, you will see a sign reading "Mower's Charge Tour Stop." Pull into the turnoff there.

N 35.20798 N 78.17632

TOUR STOP 6: Mower's Charge

You are now in the vicinity of Gen. Joseph Johnston's headquarters. the morning of March 21, Maj. Gen. Joseph Mower's division came crashing into the Confederate flank, located just your east and through woods fronting the interpretive markers.

Johnston and his staff were forced to flee. Mower now stood poised to advance into Johnston's rear and capture the Mill Creek Bridge, the only line of retreat for the Confederates. Mower, however, had advanced beyond the main Union line and was forced to shift to the south. The time it took for Mower to maneuver allowed the Confederates to rally and send in reinforcements. Attacked from three sides, Mower's understrength division was eventually forced to withdraw.

➤ TO TOUR STOP 7

Turn left back onto Westbrook Lowgrounds Road and head west approximately one-tenths of a mile. Turn right onto Devil's Racetrack Road and proceed straight ahead. You will see a wayside directly ahead of you in the fork of the road. This is the sign for the "Village of Bentonville."

N 35.208 W 78. 17638

TOUR STOP 7: **Village of Bentonville**

This is the small village of Bentonville. Confederates housed naval stores throughout the war. Many of the houses served as hospitals during the battle. Mower's Charge lurched forward, elements from the 64th Illinois Infantry entered Bentonville. The regiment was one of only

a few in the Union army that carried Henry rifles, the first lever-action repeating rifle ever produced.

Just up the road to your right and out of sight is the Mill Creek Bridge, Johnston's only line of retreat. Although the Illinoisans did not know it, they came within a breadth of capturing the bridge and trapping the Confederate army. Outdistancing their comrades, the regiment was isolated and eventually pushed back by Confederate cavalry.

PLEASE NOTE: As this volume went to press, new tour stops were under construction at the battlefield that are not included in this driving tour; please inquire at the visitor center for additional information.

Sherman's March: The Impact on Georgia and the Carolinas

APPENDIX A

BY ASHLEY WEBB

After the devastation of Atlanta in November of 1864 and the surrender of Savannah the following month, William T. Sherman started his march north into South Carolina on February 1, 1865. Continuing with the same themes involved in his troops' March to the Sea, Sherman focused on the central goal of punishing the South for its secession. The first part of this involved the issue of Special Order 120, declaring it legal to forage throughout the countryside for food, munitions, and other everyday items needed to supply the Union's advancing troops. Despite Sherman's specific orders to only take what was needed and to destroy what was necessary, Union foragers took "advantage of the license given to them," pillaging, burning, and killing unnecessarily.

The hardships Confederate citizens in Georgia and South Carolina suffered under Sherman's troops riddle letters, diaries, and memoirs, discussing in detail the atrocities enacted by Sherman's 'bummers.' One South Carolina resident categorized the organization of the foraging parties as such: "First came squads who demanded arms and whisky. Then came the rascals who hunted for silver, ransacked the ladies' wardrobes and scared women and children into fits—at least those who could be scared . . . . Then came some smiling, suave, well-dressed officers, who 'regretted it all so much.'"

With news of Union troops passing through or camping in rural areas, and rumors of Union soldiers ripping houses apart looking for valuables spread throughout the South, Confederate citizens attempted to protect their property by hiding slaves, valuables, and food. Creativity abounded as families attempted to protect their property; however, most Southerners were not lucky enough to trick the Union troops out of their spoils. No building was safe from the pilfering soldiers, and they ransacked every room from top to bottom, ripping "open mattresses and pillows, scattering feathers and cotton everywhere, and [taking] whatever they fancied."

Slave cabins received the same treatment as plantation homes: "Their cabins [were] rifled of every valuable, the

Sherman's march through Georgia and the Carolinas took him through some of the South's richest cotton country—including land still cultivated for that purpose on the Cole plantation at the Bentonville battlefield. (dd)

Millen, Georgia, burned in December of 1864. (hw)

soldiers swearing that their Sunday clothes were the white people's, and that they never had money to get such things as they had." If the family's valuables were not found after a thorough search, bummers would hang "men up on a slack rope and [poke] them with bayonets to make them tell where their valuables were hid."

Several hordes of soldiers would raid a household throughout a span of a day, and up to several times in a week. When one group left, another followed soon after, taking whatever the former had left behind until families were left destitute and starving. After a week of consistent raiding, one woman had almost nothing left for bummers to steal from her home, yet they continued to harass her family. In one of the later raids, she described her triumphant battle with a soldier over a simple household item: "A bummer took my brush and comb, I plead with him for the comb, he might have the brush, but I would be obliged to cut off my hair without a comb. . . . [I] gave a sudden grab, he held tight but I jerked it away."

Sherman's "bummer's" stripped the countryside clean. (b&l)

The houses and outbuildings were not the only spaces searched thoroughly. Soldiers systematically searched the yard and woods surrounding the house and even exhumed cemeteries looking for valuables. In South Carolina, one African American woman wept because "the recent grave of her deceased child had been dug up in the search for plunder, the tiny coffined body left discarded next to the pit." The slave remarked, "Dey won't even let de dead rest in de grave."

In addition to searching for valuables, Union foragers took any and all visible food, as well as searched every possible space for additional provisions. They often left families destitute and starving, leaving little to survive on for the rest of the winter. After hiding bits of bread and milk, which were promptly found and confiscated, one

Sherman marched his armies on review through Savannah before striking out into the Carolinas. (loc)

woman "filled a bucket with flour and . . . molasses," and told a family member to "sit on this bucket, [and] guard it well, [for] it is all there is between us and starvation."

In most cases across the South, when bummers found food, they would confiscate what they wanted, and then discard, spoil, or kill the rest. In one instance, foragers broke into one man's cellar, and after "they had drunk as much of his peach brandy as they could hold, they spit into the rest to keep the 'd - d rebels' from having it." Union foragers applied the same tactics to bags and barrels of flour, rice, grits, and other grains of which they couldn't carry on their appropriated pack animals: "They poured [our] rice and rye . . . on the dining room floor and poured molasses over the pile while flour was tracked from the barrels across the house." In another instance, soldiers "took the stopper from a barrel of syrup stored in the cellar, letting it gurgle onto the dirt floor." Cotton mills, grain storage, and other outbuildings were stripped of their yield and useful tools, and then set on fire.

Similar to looking for valuables, foragers would search vegetable gardens and orchards by "prodding the ground inch by inch" with bayonets or iron ramrods. One woman witnessed this, "I never saw anything like the slow, methodical way they went at it, but evidently they found nothing, for they next took the vegetable garden, and prodded the first vegetables up, but with no more success than in the orchard." Any meat was confiscated first, and any animals in the yard or stable were "shot down . . . and hunted as if they were rebels themselves." Even if the troops couldn't use the horses, mules, or cattle confiscated from a family, or didn't need

Sherman's men generally took livestock for the army's use, but sometimes they took animals simply to deprive the populace. (loc)

Confederates set Columbia ablaze themselves; Sherman watched it burn. (loc)

large provisions of meat, the soldiers would slaughter the animals and leave their carcasses to rot at the houses or on sides of the road. In one case, soldiers gathered up the cows, horses, mules, and other large animals they had foraged earlier, drove them to a short bend in a Georgia river, "and the order to commence firing into the poor animals began, and it was kept up as long as there was one of them left standing."

While the devastation across the south remained fairly widespread, South Carolina received the brunt of the damage. In a letter to Gen. Grant dated December 18, 1864, Sherman wrote: "we can punish South Carolina as she deserves" and planned to "devastate that State" by leaving it in shambles. And although he declared in his memoirs that he "had no malice or desire to destroy that city or its inhabitants, as is generally believed at the South," Sherman is credited with merely stating "they have brought it on themselves" when witnessing the conflagration across the city of Columbia.

Columbia was not the only city to feel the wrath of Sherman's troops. Throughout South Carolina, "isolated houses would mysteriously take fire, lighting up the line of march almost with the brilliancy of day."

As a rebuttal and in defense of his actions, Sherman dedicated several pages in his memoirs to the various activities in which bummers were engaged. "Often would I pass these foraging-parties at the roadside, waiting for their wagons to come up," he wrote, "and was amused at their strange collections—mules, horses, even cattle, packed with old saddles and loaded with hams, bacon, bags of cornmeal, and poultry of every character and description." Continuing on, he declared: "No doubt many acts of pillage, robbery, and violence, were committed by these parties of foragers. . . . for I have since heard of jewelry taken from women and the plunder of articles that never reached the commissary; but these acts were exceptional and incidental."

Regardless, the psychological and physical damage had been done, and the actions taken by Sherman and his troops instilled a deep sense of resentment and hatred toward the Union.

Based in Roanoke, Virginia, ASHLEY WEBB works as a freelance Museums Registrar and Collections Specialist. She is a regular contributor to Emerging Civil War and writes for her own blog, Blue Ridge Vintage, highlighting the history of everyday objects.

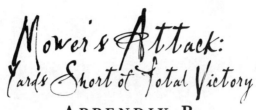

Mower's Attack: Yards Short of Total Victory

APPENDIX B
BY ROBERT M. DUNKERLY

Could one attack have influenced the ending of the war and its settlement? Perhaps.

The March 21 attack by Maj. Gen. Joseph Mower's two brigades threatened the Confederate rear and only line of retreat. With Mill Creek behind it, the Army of the South had no other way to fall back than the lone road that crossed this creek.

The attack also briefly overran Johnston's headquarters, one of the few in the war in which an army headquarters was captured. In a few fast-paced moments, Johnston's sword, belt, sash, horse, and many personal papers were swept up by the 64th Illinois.

However, quick responses by Confederate officers and an aggressive counterattack saved the day and pushed Mower's Federals back.

This situation was rare in the war: an attack on an exposed flank with the potential to totally cut off an army's line of retreat (other examples include Shiloh, Stones River, and Antietam). At any point in the war, cutting off an army's retreat and possibly destroying it would have been pivotal.

Coming in the spring of 1865, it would have been decisive.

The movement was initiated by Mower and not supported by other troops, but what if it had been? A few more divisions could have made a difference. If pushed, the Confederates would have had little room for maneuver, given their positions on March 21, and swampy ground would have made a rapid withdrawal impossible.

If Mower's attack had been larger in scale, it might have resulted in the annihilation of Johnston's army, which had nowhere to pull back to. The Army of the South could not have withdrawn and recuperated from its defeat to fight again.

A full-scale destruction of the army, resulting in a rout along the lines of the battle of Nashville, would have been disastrous for the Confederate cause. Johnston and Beauregard had spent weeks assembling this army from various and scattered commands and detachments. Its morale was fragile, its organization still embryotic. The army hadn't yet melded.

Johnston's lifeline at Bentonville: the bridge over Mill Creek. (dd)

Mower's attack as depicted in *Frank Leslie's Illustrated Newspaper.* (loc)

There are several points to ponder:

• If unable to retreat across Mill Creek, Johnston's army was trapped. The first surrender might have been here, rather than at Appomattox.

• If crushed, whether forced to surrender or not, when Lee evacuates Richmond in April, his objective is moving the Army of Northern Virginia to link up with Johnston. If the Army of the South is not in the field, this is not an option. Might there have been a surrender in the Richmond/Petersburg area rather than a final campaign westward?

• Or might Lee have advocated for a negotiated settlement when Richmond fell? He had been open to negotiations before. Davis might have had no other options, as North Carolina would have been under Federal control, preventing his flight south from Richmond.

The surrender of Johnston's army before the fall of Richmond would have put the Army of Northern Virginia in a precarious position. All of the Carolinas would lay open to Union occupation, and Virginia would be totally cut off from supply and support. In other words, Richmond and Petersburg would be untenable.

If the first surrender were here, would Lee have even attempted to continue holding out in Richmond and Petersburg? The writing would have been on the wall, if it wasn't already.

Speculation can only take us so far, and as good historians we should be open to other ideas, but not pursue them too far: there are too many variables, and too many avenues for events to unfold.

Sherman did not support Mower, and in the aftermath of the battle, he did not pursue Johnston's army. Rather, by this point, Sherman was convinced that the key to winning the war was not on the battlefield. That's why he had avoided pursuing the Army of Tennessee under Gen. John Bell Hood after the fall of Atlanta and why he made no effort to go after Confederate troops in the marches through Georgia and South Carolina. Any combat initiated in North Carolina—Averasboro and Bentonville—was initiated by Confederates who came to him.

Sherman saw targeting infrastructure, impacting civilians, and economic targets as the keys to ending the war. His focus in mid-March was on getting his forces to Goldsboro to refit and resupply.

It might be argued, however, that an aggressive counterattack at Bentonville, or a rapid pursuit of the Army of the South after it disengaged, might have brought the results that Sherman hoped for sooner.

In his memoirs, Sherman himself wrote, "With the knowledge now possessed of his small force, of course I committed an error in not overwhelming Johnston's army on the 21st of March, 1865. But I was content then to let him go . . ." Sherman was focused on the larger campaign and didn't see an opportunity to end the war sooner when it was right before him.

Perhaps another point is that Sherman underestimated Johnston's ability to cobble together an effective force so quickly. He treated it as a nuisance, when in fact it was functioning and capable of striking. That Confederate forces swept forward on March 19 and nearly overran Union troops is a testimony to Johnston, Beauregard, and their officers.

The what-ifs are endless. Would Booth still have assassinated Lincoln? Would Reconstruction have unfolded differently? Could a forced battlefield surrender of a field army have hastened the end of the war—either militarily or politically?

The troops under Mower who splashed through the swamps that March day likely had no idea how close they came to altering events.

ROBERT M. DUNKERLY *is a historian with the National Park Service and author of more than a dozen books, including the Emerging Civil War Series'* To the Bitter End: Appomattox Court House, Bennett Place, and the Surrenders of the Confederacy *and* No Turning Back: A Guide to the 1864 Overland Campaign *(with Donald C. Pfanz and David Ruth).*

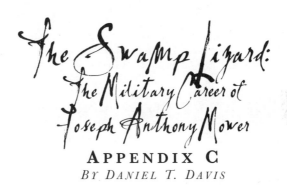

The Swamp Lizard: The Military Career of Joseph Anthony Mower

APPENDIX C
BY DANIEL T. DAVIS

When word reached Maj. Gen. William Tecumseh Sherman's headquarters on March 21, 1865, that Maj. Gen. Joseph Mower's division had broken through the Confederate left at Bentonville, it could hardly have come as a surprise. Through four years of fighting, Mower had established a reputation for being aggressive, and Sherman himself once remarked that "a better soldier or a braver man never lived than Joseph A. Mower." A Wisconsin solider who served with Mower once remarked, "We all felt that with Mower leading us, we would undertake to storm the very gates of hell and under his leadership we made good every time."

Mower was a native of Vermont and, unlike many of his contemporaries, did not attend West Point. Instead, Mower received some formal military training at Norwich Military Academy but left two years into his schooling. In 1847, Mower began his service in the United States Army during the War with Mexico when he enlisted as a private in the U.S. Engineers. At the end of the conflict, Mower was discharged and reentered civilian life.

In June 1855, Mower opted to return to the army, receiving a commission as a second lieutenant in the 1st U.S. Infantry. His conduct was impressive, and he would be promoted to captain in September 1860.

When the Southern states began to leave the Union, Mower was stationed in Texas at Camp Verde. Leaving in the face of Texas state forces, the men sailed to Key West in March, 1861. They would remain there for nearly a year before being transferred to Missouri to join Maj. Gen. John Pope's Army of the Mississippi.

Upon joining Pope, Mower's men set down their muskets to take on artillery duties. Mower commanded Pope's Siege Train and fought at New Madrid and Island Number 10. Pope's army would be transferred to Pittsburg Landing, Tennessee, to join Maj. Gen. Henry Halleck in the Federal advance on the vital crossroads town of Corinth Mississippi.

On May 3, 1862, Mower received a commission as colonel and took command of the 11th Missouri Infantry. Back in his element as an infantryman, Mower distinguished himself by leading his regiment on skirmish missions during the siege of Corinth. After the Confederates abandoned the town,

Joseph Mower led his men through this ground during his assault at Bentonville. (dd)

Mower and his regiment became part of Maj. Gen. Ulysses S. Grant's Army of the Tennessee.

That fall, Mower rose to brigade command. His men soon acquired a reputation for hard marching and became known throughout the army as "Joe Mower's Jackass Cavalry." Mower would lead his Jackasses during the hard fighting at Iuka and Corinth. On the second day of the battle of Corinth, October 4, Mower was conducting a reconnaissance when his skirmishers encountered the enemy. In the opening volleys, Mower was unhorsed and received a neck wound. Taken prisoner, Mower would later escape and return to the safety of the Union lines. Rumors, however, persisted that Mower was drunk or at least hungover that morning, and his incapacitated state contributed to his capture. Interestingly, these accusations did not carry much weight with his superiors, and Mower was promoted to brigadier general in March 1863.

Mower and his brigade would participate in Grant's Vicksburg campaign. When the Federals captured Jackson, Mississippi, Mower was made provost marshal of the town. On May 22, 1863, Mower's brigade assaulted the Stockade Redan. Although he was repulsed, Mower's conduct impressed his corps commander, Maj. Gen. William Tecumseh Sherman. The following spring, Mower's brigade participated in Sherman's Meridian expedition, guarding the Union wagon train.

Rising to division command, Mower transferred to Maj. Gen. Andrew J. Smith's XVI Corps and participated in the Red River expedition, where Mower distinguished himself again—this time during the storming and capture of Fort De Russy. Later in the summer, Mower fought at Tupelo, Mississippi. On August 12, 1864, Mower received a promotion to the rank of major general and served in Missouri during Sterling Price's invasion.

Mower's earlier actions, however, had not been forgotten. Preparing to march from Atlanta to the Atlantic Coast, Sherman requested that Mower accompany his armies. Mower returned to the Army of the Tennessee and commanded a division in the XVII Corps during the "March to the Sea."

When Sherman left Savannah to begin his march into the Carolinas, Mower's division engaged the Confederates as they moved through the low country swamps. Major General Oliver O. Howard, who was with Mower's division, recalled: "His energy in leading his men . . . and directing them . . . was marvelous and

Joseph Mower was no stranger to nicknames. While he would become known as the "Swamp Lizard" during the Carolinas Campaign, Mower had acquired another nickname earlier in the war. After conducting a reconnaissance and safely withdrawing his men in the face of a large enemy force at Iuka, Mississippi, in the fall of 1862, he was dubbed "the Wolf." Additionally, the brigade Mower commanded throughout 1862 and into 1863 was known as the "Eagle Brigade"—a nickname derived from a bald eagle, Old Abe, that served as the regimental mascot of the 8th Wisconsin. (loc)

drew my attention more than ever to his capabilities."
One particular morning, Mower awoke with his clothing
covered in icicles, encouraging his men to give him the
sobriquet "Swamp Lizard."

At Bentonville, after repositioning his division on
the Union right, Mower sent his infantrymen crashing
into the enemy left. The assault
shattered the Confederate line
and Mower came within a
breath of cutting the Rebel line
of retreat. Unsupported and
under orders to return to the
main line, Mower was eventually
driven back after multiple
counterattacks. Although
Sherman would call the action
"rash," he would write later in
life of his regret in not following
up Mower's attack.

**Mower (seated, center)
surrounded by his staff.** (loc)

Shortly after the battle, Mower was elevated to
command of the XX Corps in the Army of Georgia.
Bentonville would prove to be his last major battle as the
various Confederate armies began to capitulate in the
spring of 1865.

Following the war, Mower commanded the all-black
39th U.S. Infantry before transferring to head another
black unit, the 25th U.S. Infantry. He would later
take command of the Department of Louisiana with
headquarters in New Orleans. Mower would pass away
from pneumonia there on January 6, 1870. He rests in
Arlington National Cemetery. Of his actions during
the Civil War, Sherman would state, "I can recall many
instances when he displayed abilities of the highest order,
entitling him to the full name and fame of General."

The Unity Monument a
Bennett Place. (cm

The Road to Bennett Place

APPENDIX D
BY CHRIS MACKOWSKI

For William T. Sherman and Joe Johnston, the road to Bennett Place started in Manassas, Virginia. Unlike the two army commanders, though, I've come here to north-central North Carolina, to the outskirts of Durham, with intent rather than through happenstance.

I've come here to listen to *them*.

Sherman and Johnston found themselves on opposite sides at that great opening battle, Sherman as a colonel in command of a brigade of three-month volunteers and Johnston as commander of all Confederate forces.

From there, the war took them on different paths until the spring of 1864, when they clashed again outside Atlanta. By then, Sherman commanded all Union troops in the Western theater. Johnston, who'd been shuffled from command to command because of his poor relationship with Confederate President Jefferson Davis, had landed with the Army of Tennessee.

Sherman's forces far outnumbered Johnston's, who nonetheless led a skillful defensive campaign, although it eventually got him fired. Months later, after Sherman batted around Johnston's replacement and then ran roughshod over Georgia and South Carolina, Johnston came back to command for a final round. While he struck a blow at Bentonville, Johnston knew there wasn't much he could do to stop Sherman unless he united with Robert E. Lee's beleaguered Army of Northern Virginia. Lee's surrender to Grant at Appomattox made that option moot.

So that he could negotiate from strength, Johnston kept his own army together and far from Sherman's reach. He hoped to secure terms for his men more favorable than the ones offered to Lee. Sherman, for his part, feared that Johnston would disperse his army into the mountains and carry on the war as a guerilla campaign—an option Sherman saw as disastrous—so he sought to do whatever he could to avoid that.

After a few rounds of shuttle diplomacy, the two men met along a forest road near Durham, midway between Johnston's HQ in Greensboro and Sherman's HQ in Raleigh. When Sherman asked Johnston if he knew of a place where they could confer privately, Johnston suggested a small farmhouse he and his staff had just passed.

The Bennett farmhouse has been restored to look today much as it did in 1865. (cm)

The home, owned by 59-year-old James Bennett—also spelled Bennitt—was a modest two-story building with a spacious common room, where the two generals sat down to hammer out terms. The pall of President Lincoln's assassination hung over the table, but Sherman nonetheless offered sweepingly generous terms. He and Johnston sought to take matters even further by arranging "the terms of a permanent peace."

Sherman had no way of knowing that northern sentiment, hostile in the wake of Lincoln's murder, would turn against him and his magnanimous offer. In fact, the terms were so generous, yet sentiment so rancorous, that Union General-in-Chief Ulysses S. Grant was forced to pay a personal visit to his trusted subordinate, Sherman.

In the end, Sherman was forced to revise his offer so that it mirrored the terms Grant had extended at Appomattox, although Sherman also agreed to a supplementary set of conditions for Johnston's men.

Sherman and Johnston met a total of three times at the Bennett's farmhouse as they worked to finalize their agreement. On April 26, both men put pen to paper. Johnston surrendered all Confederate forces in the Carolinas, Georgia, and Florida—more than 89,000 in all—making it the largest surrender of the war.

It was not the last surrender, though. Richard Taylor would surrender in Alabama on May 4, Edmund Kirby Smith would surrender Trans-Mississippi forces on May 26, and Stand Watie would surrender in Indian Territory on June 23. The Confederate raider *Shenandoah* wouldn't surrender until August.

*   *   *

The grand vision for peace Sherman and Johnston

shared was commemorated at the site in 1923 with a memorial. Two columns support a block that says "Unity." A bronze tablet, featuring a picture of the Bennett farmhouse, recounts the story.

The farmhouse burned down in 1921, although the stone chimney survived. In the 1960s, to coincide with the Civil War's centennial, the state of North Carolina reconstructed the farmhouse based on photographs and wartime sketches. The state now operates the facility as a state historic site.

The Bennett farmhouse offered a beautiful backdrop for the surrender negotiations. (NCDAH)

The original road trace, lined by a snake-rail fence, still runs past the farmhouse. A kitchen and smokehouse stand nearby, and a fenced-in garden and a livestock corral, empty, sit quietly beyond.

As I walk from the visitor center, I noticed that I have the place to myself. Earlier, before I'd watched the orientation film and visited the small museum, a docent had led a handful of tourists around the property. Now they're as gone as the armies.

Fortunately, Bennett Place speaks for itself. I can hear its voices in the crunch of the gravel roadbed beneath my cowboy boots, the hollow clunk of the farmhouse's front door when it closes, the imagined sound of footfalls on the house's plank floor.

Some of the voices, like cavalry rivals Wade Hampton and Judson Kilpatrick, seethe and burn and snarl. Others, like Johnston's, are quiet, firm, authoritative or, like Sherman's, gruff yet reasonable—and, mayhaps, even pleasant.

As "Old Joe" Johnston and "Uncle Billy" Sherman sat at a Quaker-simple table, they affixed their names to bold, hopeful ideas. I can hear them talking still.

Bennett Place reminds me to share their optimism.

Because if Bennett Place is a place of surrender—of ending—it is also a place of beginning. Peace and unity began here, as did a long friendship between Johnston and Sherman. The two generals, who'd earned each other's respect during their campaigns against each other, remained friends for the rest of their lives.

That is how peace and unity begin.

Bennett Place represents such unceremonial magnitude: the largest surrender of the war, the grandest vision for peace, the enduring bonds of friendship, the challenge of unity.

What could be bigger than all that?

What could be bigger than the future?

CHRIS MACKOWSKI, Ph.D., is the editor of Emerging Civil War and the author of a dozen books.

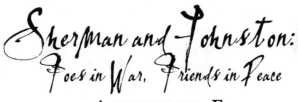

Sherman and Johnston:
Foes in War, Friends in Peace

APPENDIX E
BY PHILLIP S. GREENWALT

From a small wooden cabin outside Durham, North Carolina, to the streets of New York City, one of the enduring legacies of the last campaign of the Civil War was the lifelong relationship between the two army commanders.

Joseph E. Johnston and William T. Sherman had fought against each other from the opening salvos at First Manassas to the arid climate of northern Mississippi, to the red clay of northern Georgia, all the way to the last death throes of the Confederacy in North Carolina.

From their divergent paths as adversaries came a grudging respect that spawned a kindred friendship that lasted until the day Sherman died on February 14, 1891.

That respect the two generals developed had its roots in their first face-to-face encounter, on April 26, 1865, when the Ohioan Sherman met with the Virginian Johnston in the small homestead of James and Nancy Bennett, approximately six miles to the northwest of Durham, North Carolina. Johnston was bent on doing the honorable thing, especially after Robert E. Lee's surrender in Virginia on April 9. He was on record as stating that further resistance by his forces after the surrender at Appomattox Court House would be "criminal." However, that deal fell through when the authorities in Washington, D.C., rejected it. Johnston stayed true to his word to surrender, though, ignoring the insistence of Confederate President Jefferson Davis, who wanted to continue the struggle. That earned Sherman's respect.

The cordiality of Sherman and Johnston's meeting reflected their resolve to help reconcile the officers and men of their respective commands to peace. All around them, nerves were strained and tensions high—best exemplified by their two cavalry commanders, Union Maj. Gen. Judson Kilpatrick and Confederate Lt. Gen. Wade Hampton, who almost came to blows outside the farmhouse as the commanders hashed out their peace agreement inside. Sherman and Johnston emerged from the Bennett House just in time to calm their subordinates. The first test of their respectful post-war relationship kept another round of fighting from erupting.

Johnston and Sherman negotiated the terms of surrender at the Bennett's table. Their meeting there led to a friendship that lasted the rest of their lives. (cm)

In the years after the war, the Bennet farmstead fell into disrepair even as the relationship between the two generals who met there flourished. (loc)

Although they separated after their meeting outside Durham, their paths would cross again in the future. Sherman continued in the military and took over as general in chief in 1869, assuming the top billing in the military from his friend Ulysses S. Grant. In February 1884, Sherman retired from the military and initially resided in St. Louis, Missouri. He moved to New York City two years after his retirement and dabbled in the arts, chiefly painting and the theater. He was also active on a speaking tour about his war experiences.

Importantly, Sherman was also one of the first of the general officers to write his memoirs and reminiscences of his role in the American Civil War. With that writing, Sherman put down for posterity the respect he had for Johnston, calling him a "wily opponent." Published to wide acclaim in 1889, the memoirs reflected the wide reconciliationist sentiments of the time, establishing Sherman and Johnston as opponents who earned each other's grudging admiration.

Grant, too, would provide some respectful insights into Johnston's military decisions and actions in his memoirs. Johnston's 1864 campaign in Georgia had been a lightning rod for criticism from Davis supporters and by Johnston's replacement, Lt. Gen. John Bell Hood, yet Grant defended Johnston's strategy "right," worrying that it "could have prolonged the war" for even a "year beyond the time that it finally did close," which could have been catastrophic to the North's chances of winning the contest.

Johnston fared better in the opinions of his former adversaries than he did in the company of his former cohorts in the Confederacy, though. The bitterness between Johnston and Davis did not end with the conclusion of the war but spilled into magazine articles. When Johnston published his memoirs, Davis balked. "Johnston has more effectively than another could shown his selfishness and his malignity," the former Confederate president said. This began a multi-year writing campaign between the two men, which escalated into the writings of former Confederates like Hood, who had a disparaging view of Johnston, and P.G.T. Beauregard, who took umbrage with the way Johnston downplayed his contribution on the field of First Manassas. Johnston's image through much of the South suffered as a result of the controversy.

"The testimony of an enemy in one's favor" can be "worth more than that of a friend," he had written in his Narrative of Military Operations. Both Sherman, who praised the cunningness of Johnston's generalship, and Grant, who validated the Virginian's decision-making in the fateful 1863 Vicksburg Campaign, had vindicated his controversial career.

Johnston repaid Sherman's magnanimity by meeting with the general for frequent dinners when Sherman visited the capital. Johnston was, by that time, serving in Washington as a Democratic congressman from Virginia. According to one biographer, the old Virginian would never consent to hearing Sherman—reviled in much of the South—spoken ill of in his presence for his remaining days.

The final show of respect came in the dreary and cold drizzle of mid-February 1891 in New York City. Sherman passed away rather unexpectedly after complaining for a few days that he didn't feel well; one account suggests that the asthma that plagued him throughout his life contributed to his death. Johnston traveled north to be one of the honorary pallbearers for the casket of his late friend. With rain pelting down, Johnston stood at the graveside with his hat removed as a sign of respect. Someone leaned in to the ear of the former Confederate general and, with grave concern for the general's health, inquired whether Johnston should put his hat back on to lessen the chance of catching a cold himself.

Sherman (left) and Johnston (right) in their later years. (loc)

The rigid, respectful, and obstinate old man replied: "If I were in his place and he was standing here in mine, he would not put on his hat."

That settled the question then and there.

Johnston did develop a cold, though—which, by the time he ventured back to Washington D.C., had turned into pneumonia. Thirty-five days later, the Virginian himself passed away. The next day, to show the respect Johnston had garnered from former enemies, John M. Schofield and William Rosecrans paid their respects.

Sherman had been 71 years old when he passed the previous month; Johnston was 84.

In death, their bodies went opposite routes from their Civil War service: Sherman's body was sent southwest to be interred in the family plot at Calvary Cemetery in St. Louis, where his wife was interred; Johnston's remains headed north from Washington D.C. to be buried in Green Mount Cemetery in Baltimore, Maryland, next to his own wife.

A former soldier under Johnston, Sam Watkins, best known for his memoir, "Co. Aytch," gave a fitting epitaph for his old commander. Although biographers have used it for Johnston ever since, it just as well sums up the respect the rank-and-file had for both Sherman and Johnston: "We privates loved you because you made us love ourselves."

Sherman may be best known for his epithet that "War is hell"—a course he pursued until he met Johnston across a small wooden table in a small wooden home in North Carolina. But from that "hell," a friendship was spawned that intertwined the two men for the rest of their lives.

Shortly after Sherman's death in 1891, members of the Society of the Army of the Tennessee—men whom Sherman had led and fought with throughout the war—began plans for an equestrian statue to their chief. With the help of Congress, it was completed in 1903; on October 15, President Theodore Roosevelt spoke at the dedication. The statue, which sits in President's Park near the White House, cost nearly $124,000 and was designed by sculptor Carl Rohl-Smith, who died before it was finished; sculptor Lauritz Jensen and others finished the work. Directly below Sherman stand four soldiers representing the branches of the army: an infantryman, cavalryman, artilleryman, and engineer. The engagements in which Sherman participated are etched along the base. The inscription on the base is a quote from their beloved Uncle Billy: "On no earthly account will I do any act or think any thought hostile to or in defiance of the old government of the United States." (loc)

Preserving the Bentonville Battlefield

APPENDIX F
BY DONNY TAYLOR

The battle of Bentonville, March 19, 20, and 21, 1865, was the only major effort to stop Gen. William T. Sherman's advance through the Carolinas. After three days of battle, Gen. Joseph Johnston's Confederate army withdrew northward towards Smithfield while Sherman continued his march towards Goldsboro, North Carolina, ending the largest battle ever fought on North Carolina soil.

In the years after the battle, the citizens of Bentonville put their lives back together, farmed the land, rebuilt the buildings destroyed or damaged during the battle, and raised their families. The battle was not forgotten, however, as the woods and fields are now preserved as hallowed ground where men of both armies shed blood, performing their duty to their country.

The first efforts to memorialize the battle began in 1894 by the Goldsboro Rifles, a post war militia unit and the namesake of Company A, 27th North Carolina Troops 1861-1865. In 1894, they began an effort to raise money to place a monument on the property of John Harper in the Bentonville community along the Old Goldsboro Road. After a year of fundraising, these efforts came to fruition on March 20, 1895—the 30th anniversary of the battle. The keynote address on this occasion was given by former Confederate general Wade Hampton, who 30-years prior had developed the battle plan that General Johnston approved. The monument unveiled to the public was an obelisk that contained many names of Confederate soldiers killed or wounded during the battle.

It was not until 1927 that another monument was placed on the battlefield, this time by the North Carolina United Daughters of the Confederacy and the North Carolina Historical Commission. This monument was dedicated to the North Carolina Junior Reserves, the "seed corn of the Confederacy," which fought gallantly during the battle. The monument is a bronze tablet set in Wake County granite and placed at the intersection of Harper House Road and Bass Road, the position occupied by these young boys.

A monument to the soldiers and civilians on North Carolina affected by the battle of Bentonville. (dd)

Once the well-attended ceremony was over,

the battlefield once again became a quiet farming community for many years. Nearly 40 years later, the state of Texas placed a pink granite monument to the Texas regiments that were in the battle during the battle's 100th anniversary commemoration in 1965. In 1992 the Harper House Bentonville Chapter of the United Daughters of the Confederacy placed a large rectangular monument resembling a tomb to honor the North Carolina soldiers and loved ones.

An attempt to place a monument to the Union soldiers at Bentonville began in 1993 but was not passed by the North Carolina Historical Commission. That effort was renewed in 2012 by the Sons of Union Veterans, General Thomas Ruger Camp #1, to place a monument at Bentonville to honor the four Union Corps in the battle. This time the effort was successful, and a granite monument was dedicated on the 148th anniversary of the battle in March 2013.

Interest in making Bentonville Battlefield a historic site was heightened in the 1950s by the approaching Civil War centennial commemorations. Attention was focused on the Harper house, once owned by John and Amy Harper. The house served as a XIV Corps Union hospital and treated approximately 600 wounded men, both Union and Confederate. In 1957, Mr. Herschel Rose and the Harper House/Bentonville Chapter UDC led efforts for battlefield preservation. That year, the North Carolina General Assembly appropriated $25,000.00 for the purchase of the Harper house and 51 acres of land surrounding the home. The home and property were purchased that year from Mr. J. J. Dunn, and the Bentonville Battleground Association raised and additional $15,000.00 to restore the home to its wartime appearance. Also during that period of time, the Bentonville Battleground Association was superseded by the Bentonville Battleground Advisory Committee with the primary purpose to seek funding for a visitor center.

In 1961 the North Carolina General Assembly appropriated $26,000.00 for a visitor's center. The Bentonville Battleground Advisory Committee raised an additional $14,000.00 through foundation gifts and private donations. Construction began on the Visitor Center in January 1964 and was completed in June of that year. The official dedication occurred during the centennial on March 21, 1965.

Little activity other than normal visitation and some small-scale reenactments occurred at Bentonville during the 1970s through the mid-1980s. The first steps toward in-depth interpretive programming did not begin until 1986, which also coincided with the first acquisitions of battlefield property. Thirty-six acres were purchased, which included a section of the Army of Tennessee earthworks with remnants of revetment logs still visible. These efforts continued through the 1990s with small tracts of land being purchased with the help of the Association for the Preservation of Civil War Sites (APCWS), Bentonville Battlefield Historical Association, Inc. (BBHA), and donations.

The catalyst for large-scale preservation began with the Congressionally mandated American Battlefield Protection Program's (ABPP) Civil War Battlefield Survey, which brought Bentonville to the attention of the National Park Service (NPS). Bentonville became a Priority 1-Class A battlefield. A nomination application for National Historic Landmark designation was prepared and submitted, and in 1996 Bentonville received National Landmark status. This expanded the battlefield's ability to apply for federal grants to help fund property purchases. During that time Bentonville was placed as one of the most deserving battlefields, thus given the highest priority for preservation action.

A cannon sits behind earthworks near the Bentonville visitor center. (cm)

As small parcels of property began being added to the battlefield, something needed to be in place to designate priority areas of the battlefield and its resources. The Bentonville Battleground Preservation Plan, sponsored by the BBHA, the ABPP, and the NPS, was published in 1998 by the Jaeger Company. This was an in-depth study of the entire 6,000-acre battlefield. Included are study boundary areas and primary engagement areas for each day of the battle. This also covers historical resources and significance, property owners, prioritized parcels, greenways, and tour trails. This publication is still used today in planning, implementing purchases, and preservation efforts.

The Bentonville Battlefield Resources Final Report was published by the National Park Services in 2000. This report uses information from the Global Positioning Systems (GPS) to locate and plot on maps all the existing earthworks and features of the battlefield and the conditions of the remaining earthworks.

These publications have proven to be an invaluable resource in both locating and documenting areas for purchase and or interpretation. The information found in these reports led directly to the purchase of important battlefield parcels that had been previously overlooked.

Members of the North Carolina Civil War Roundtable (pictured here touring the battlefield) have raised more than $15,500 to help preserve Bentonville. With matching funds available through the Civil War Trust, that amount has been parlayed into more than $511,000 toward preservation.
(ga)

The purchase of historical acreage began in earnest in 2001 with the addition of two properties, followed by two more with trenches in 2002. In 2003, work began with the Civil War Preservation Trust, now the Civil War Trust, and through that relationship the protected property has expanded from approximately 200 acres in 2001 to more than 2,000 acres at present. This does not include properties now under contract and other designated tracts for future additions to the site. Major funding for these purchases has come from many organizations and individuals over the years, many more than can be listed in the document. All these donations and gifts have enabled the expansion and interpretation of the battlefield.

Today at Bentonville Battlefield, we use the property expansion for many purposes. Much of the property remains as farmland, which is rented to local farmers. The revenue from the rent remains here at the battlefield, providing funding for temporary employees and maintenance to the site. The farmers are also another set of eyes on the battlefield and notify the staff of any signs of trespassing or illegal artifact collecting.

We have installed tour stops throughout the battlefield that include interpretive panels with battle maps, a short history of that area, and quotes from soldiers on that part of the field. To accompany these panels, we have a cell phone audio tour that gives approximately a five-minute narration about that sector of the battle.

Also in progress is a walking tour of approximately three miles. This tour takes the visitor from the visitor center through the battle of March 19 along both Union and Confederate earthworks, ending at the Junior Reserve Tour Stop. Along the line of battle, brigade markers will be placed to correspond with unit positions on the battle maps. We are also working with

Howell Woods Environmental Learning Center, a part of Johnston County Community College, to enhance the walking trail and expand the interpretation to include information about the flora and fauna of the battlefield. Once this trail is completed, future plans are to loop the trail south of the Harper House Road to interpret the battle below the road and return to the visitor center.

Two Ground Penetrating Radar (GPR) surveys have been performed at Bentonville. The first survey, followed by an archaeological dig, located the 1895 reburials of the

Historic Site Supervisor Donny Taylor shows off a section of earthworks on land purchased with donations from the North Carolina Civil War Roundtable; NCCWR past treasurer Tommy Cole joins him. (ga)

Confederate soldiers that died at the Harper house. Once this was located, the Harper House/Bentonville UDC funded 22 Confederate headstones, and each grave was properly marked. A GPR study and archaeological dig was also performed behind the Harper house in hope of finding any period support structures for the farm. A couple of interesting locations were found that will need more study.

Visitation has steadily increased each year, and it is an exciting time to work at Bentonville Battlefield. The land expansion gives us many more opportunities to develop the interpretation and allow visitors to get up close to where the fighting occurred. Bentonville Battlefield now offers an audio-visual program, a fiber optic battle map, a gift shop, and guided tours of the Harper house and dependencies. Self-guided tours of the Harper family and Confederate cemeteries, monument area, tour trail, and battlefield are also available. Private guided battlefield tours are available for groups for a fee with advanced notice. Military staff rides are very popular at Bentonville, for which we never charge a fee.

Throughout this article you may have noticed Bentonville Battleground or Battlefield being used. It was initially a battleground but was officially changed to battlefield in 2003 to differentiate it from Revolutionary War battlegrounds in North Carolina. Battlefield also seems to be the term used most commonly for Civil War battles.

Bentonville Battlefield State Historic Site is a part of the North Carolina Department of Cultural Resources, Division of Historic Sites.

DONNY TAYLOR *is the historic site manager for the* **Bentonville Battlefield State Historic Site.**

THE BATTLE OF BENTONVILLE

Combined Union Army Commander
Maj. Gen. William T. Sherman

Headquarters Guard 7th Company, Ohio Sharpshooters
Engineers and Mechanics *1st Michigan · 1st Missouri (five companies)*

ARMY OF THE TENNESSEE (RIGHT WING)
Maj. Gen. Oliver O. Howard

Escort: *15th Illinois Cavalry · 4th Company Ohio Cavalry*
Pontoon Train Guard: *14th Wisconsin (Company E)*

FIFTEENTH ARMY CORPS Maj. Gen. John A. Logan
FIRST DIVISION Bvt. Maj. Gen. Charles R. Woods
First Brigade Bvt. Brig. Gen. William B. Woods
12th Indiana · 26th Iowa · 27th Missouri · 31st & 32nd Missouri (six companies)
76th Ohio

Second Brigade Col. Robert F. Catterson
26th Illinois · 40th Illinois · 103rd Illinois · 97th Indiana · 100th Indiana · 6th Iowa
46th Ohio

Third Brigade Col. George A. Stone
4th Iowa · 9th Iowa · 25th Iowa · 30th Iowa · 31st Iowa

SECOND DIVISION Maj. Gen. William B. Hazen
First Brigade Col. Theodore Jones
55th Illinois · 116th Illinois · 127th Illinois · 6th Missouri (Companies A & B,
8th Missouri also attached) · 30th Ohio · 57th Ohio

Second Brigade Col. Wells S. Jones
11th Illinois · 83rd Indiana · 37th Ohio · 47th Ohio · 53rd Ohio · 54th Ohio

Third Brigade Brig. Gen. John M. Oliver
48th Illinois · 90th Illinois · 99th Indiana · 15th Michigan · 70th Ohio

THIRD DIVISION Bvt. Maj. Gen. John E. Smith
First Brigade Brig. Gen. T. Clark
*63rd Illinois · 93rd Illinois (with non-veterans detachment of 18th Wisconsin) · 48th Indiana
59th Indiana · 4th Minnesota*

Second Brigade Col. Clark R. Wever
*56th Illinois · 10th Iowa · 17th Iowa (one company)
26th Missouri (two companies & detachment 10th Missouri) · 80th Ohio*

FOURTH DIVISION Bvt. Maj. Gen. John M. Corse
First Brigade Brig. Gen. Elliott W. Rice
52nd Illinois · 66th Indiana · 2nd Iowa · 7th Iowa

Second Brigade Col. Robert N. Adams
12th Illinois · 66th Illinois · 81st Ohio

Third Brigade Col. Frederick J. Hurlbut
7th Illinois · 50th Illinois · 57th Illinois · 39th Iowa

Unassigned
110th United States Colored Troops

Artillery Lt. Col. William H. Ross
*1st Illinois Light, Battery H (DeGress) · 1st Michigan Light, Battery B (Wright's) ·
1st Missouri Light, Battery H (Callahan's) · 12th Wisconsin Battery (Zickerick's)*

SEVENTEENTH ARMY CORPS Maj. Gen. Frank P. Blair, Jr.
Escort: *11th Illinois Cavalry (Company G)*

FIRST DIVISION Maj. Gen. Joseph A. Mower
First Brigade Brig. Gen. John W. Fuller
64th Illinois · 18th Missouri · 27th Ohio · 39th Ohio

Second Brigade Col. Milton Montgomery
35th New Jersey · 43rd Ohio · 63rd Ohio · 25th Wisconsin[1]

Third Brigade Col. John Tillson
10th Illinois · 25th Indiana · 32nd Wisconsin

THIRD DIVISION Brig. Gen. Manning F. Force
Provost Guard: *20th Illinois*
First Brigade Col. Cassius Fairchild
30th Illinois · 31st Illinois · 45th Illinois · 12th Wisconsin · 16th Wisconsin

Second Brigade Col. Greenberry F. Wiles
20th Ohio · 68th Ohio · 78th Ohio · 17th Wisconsin

FOURTH DIVISION Bvt. Maj. Gen. Giles A. Smith
First Brigade Brig. Gen. Benjamin F. Potts
14th/15th Illinois (battalion) · 53rd Illinois · 23rd Indiana · 53rd Indiana · 32nd Ohio

Second Brigade Brig. Gen. William W. Belknap
32nd Illinois · 11th Iowa · 13th Iowa · 15th Iowa · 6th Iowa

Artillery Maj. Allen C. Waterhouse
1st Michigan Light, Battery C · 1st Minnesota Battery · 159th Ohio Battery

Unassigned
9th Illinois (mounted)

ARMY OF GEORGIA (LEFT WING)
Maj. Gen. William W. Slocum
Pontoniers: *58th Indiana*

FOURTEENTH ARMY CORPS Bvt. Maj. Gen. Jefferson C. Davis
FIRST DIVISION Brig. Gen. William P. Carlin
First Brigade Bvt. Brig. Gen. Harrison C. Hobart
104th Illinois · 88th Indiana · 33rd Ohio · 94th Ohio · 21st Wisconsin · 42nd Indiana

Second Brigade Bvt. Brig. Gen. George P. Buell
13th Michigan · 21st Michigan · 69th Ohio

Third Brigade Lt. Col. David Miles[2], Lt. Col. Arnold McMahan
38th Indiana · 21st Ohio · 74th Ohio[3] · 79th Pennsylvania

SECOND DIVISION Brig. Gen. James D. Morgan
Provost Guard *110th Illinois (Company B with Company A, 24th Illinois attached)*
First Brigade Brig. Gen. William Vandever
16th Illinois · 60th Illinois · 10th Michigan · 14th Michigan · 17th New York

Second Brigade Brig. Gen. John G. Mitchell
34th Illinois · 78th Illinois · 98th Ohio · 108th Ohio · 113th Ohio · 121st Ohio

Third Brigade Bvt. Brig. Gen. Benjamin D. Fearing[4], Lt. Col. James W. Langley
86th Illinois · 125th Illinois · 22nd Indiana · 37th Indiana (one company) · 52nd Ohio
85th Illinois[5]

THIRD DIVISION Bvt. Maj. Gen. Absalom Baird[6]
First Brigade Col. Morton C. Hunter
82nd Indiana · 23rd Missouri (four companies) · 17th Ohio · 31st Ohio · 89th Ohio · 92nd Ohio (11th Ohio attached)

Second Brigade Lt. Col. Thomas Doan
75th Indiana · 87th Indiana · 101st Indiana · 2nd Minnesota · 105th Ohio

Third Brigade Col. George P. Este
74th Indiana · 18th Kentucky · 14th Ohio · 38th Ohio

Artillery Maj. Charles Houghtaling
1st Illinois Light, Battery C (Scovel's) · 2nd Illinois Light, Battery I (Rich's) · 19th Indiana Battery (Webb's) · 5th Wisconsin Battery (McKnight's)

TWENTIETH ARMY CORPS Bvt. Maj. Gen. Alpheus S. Williams
FIRST DIVISION Brig. Gen. Nathaniel J. Jackson
First Brigade Col. James L. Selfridge
5th Connecticut · 123rd New York · 141st New York · 46th Pennsylvania

Second Brigade Col. William Hawley
2nd Massachusetts · 13th New Jersey · 107th New York · 150th New York · 3rd Wisconsin

Third Brigade Brig. Gen. James S. Robinson
82nd Illinois · 101st Illinois · 143rd New York · 61st Ohio · 82nd Ohio · 31st Wisconsin

SECOND DIVISION Bvt. Maj. Gen. John W. Geary[7]
First Brigade Bvt. Brig. Gen. Ario Pardee, Jr.
5th Ohio · 29th Ohio · 66th Ohio · 28th Pennsylvania · 147th Pennsylvania

Second Brigade Col. George W. Mindil
33rd New Jersey · 73rd Pennsylvania · 109th Pennsylvania · 119th New York · 134th New York · 154th New York

Third Brigade Bvt. Brig. Gen. Henry A. Barnum
60th New York · 102nd New York · 137th New York · 149th New York · 29th Pennsylvania · 111th Pennsylvania

THIRD DIVISION Bvt. Maj. Gen. William T. Ward
First Brigade Col. Henry Case
70th Indiana · 79th Ohio · 102nd Illinois · 105th Illinois · 129th Illinois

Second Brigade Col. Daniel Dustin
33rd Indiana · 85th Indian · 19th Michigan · 22nd Wisconsin

Third Brigade Bvt. Brig. Gen. William Cogswell
20th Connecticut · 33rd Massachusetts · 55th Ohio · 73rd Ohio · 26th Wisconsin · 136th New York

Artillery Maj. John A. Reynolds
1st New York Light, Battery I (Winegar's) · 1st New York Light, Battery M (Newkirk's) · 1st Ohio Light, Battery C (Stephens') · Pennsylvania Light, Battery E (Sloan's)[8]

CAVALRY
THIRD DIVISION Bvt. Maj. Gen. Judson Kilpatrick
First Brigade Col. Thomas J. Jordan
3rd Indiana Battalion · 8th Indiana · 2nd Kentucky · 3rd Kentucky · 9th Pennsylvania

Second Brigade Bvt. Brig. Gen. Smith D. Atkins
92nd Illinois (mounted) · 9th Ohio · 10th Ohio · 9th Michigan McLaughlin's Squadron (Ohio)

Third Brigade Col. George E. Spencer
1st Alabama · 5th Kentucky · 5th Ohio

Fourth Brigade-provisional Lt. Col. William B. Way[9]
1st Regiment · 2nd Regiment · 3rd Regiment

Artillery
10th Wisconsin Battery (Beebe's)

* * *

1 *25th Wisconsin only regiment to see action at Bentonville; the rest were assigned as a train guard*
2 *Wounded March 19*
3 *Was in the rear acting as train guard during battle of Bentonville*
4 *Wounded March 19*
5 *Was in the rear acting as train guard during battle of Bentonville*
6 *Was in the rear acting as train guard on March 19 but arrived on the battlefield on March 20, minus the Third Brigade which continued on train guard through the battle of Bentonville*
7 *Remained in the rear as a train guard on March 19; the First & Third Brigades reach the battlefield March 20*
8 *Sloan's Battery will arrive on the field at Bentonville on March 20, with the Geary's Division*
9 *Comprised of dismounted men from the Third Division, with the regimental numbers coinciding with what parent brigade the soldiers had been part of*

Confederate Army of the South
Gen. Joseph E. Johnston

ARMY OF TENNESSEE
Lt. Gen. Alexander P "A. P." Stewart

LEE'S CORPS Maj. Gen. Daniel Harvey "D. H." Hill
STEVENSON'S DIVISION Maj. Gen. Carter L. Stevenson
Palmer's Brigade Brig. Gen. Joseph B. Palmer
3rd Tennessee · 18th Tennessee · 26th Tennessee · 32nd Tennessee · 45th Tennessee
46th Tennessee · 58th North Carolina · 60th North Carolina · 54th Virginia · 63rd Virginia
23rd Tennessee Battalion

Pettus' Brigade Brig. Gen. Edmund W. Pettus[1]
20th Alabama · 23rd Alabama · 30th Alabama · 31st Alabama · 46th Alabama

Cummings' Brigade Col. Robert J. Henderson[2]
34th Georgia · 36th Georgia · 39th Georgia · 56th Georgia

CLAYTON'S DIVISION Maj. Gen. Henry D. Clayton
Stovall's Brigade Col. Henry C. Kellogg
40th Georgia · 41st Georgia · 42nd Georgia · 43rd Georgia · 52nd Georgia

Jackson's Brigade Lt. Col. Osceola Kyle
25th Georgia · 29th Georgia · 30th Georgia · 66th Georgia · 1st Confederate
1st Battalion Georgia Sharpshooters

Baker's Brigade Brig. Gen. Alpheus Baker
37th Alabama · 40th Alabama · 42nd Alabama · 54th Alabama

HILL'S DIVISION Col. Jacob G. Coltart
Deas' Brigade Col. Harry T. Toulmin
19th Alabama · 22nd Alabama · 25th Alabama · 39th Alabama · 50th Alabama

Manigault's Brigade Lt. Col. John C. Carter
24th Alabama · 34th Alabama · 10th South Carolina · 19th South Carolina

STEWART'S CORPS Maj. Gen. William W. Loring
LORING'S DIVISION Col. James Jackson
Adams' Brigade Lt. Col. Robert J. Lawrence
6th Mississippi · 14th Mississippi · 15th Mississippi[3] · 20th Mississippi
23rd Mississippi · 43rd Mississippi

Scott's Brigade Capt. John A. Dixon
27th Alabama · 35th Alabama · 49th Alabama · 55th Alabama · 57th Alabama · 12th Louisiana

Featherston's Brigade Maj. Martin A. Oatis
1st Mississippi · 3rd Mississippi · 22nd Mississippi · 31st Mississippi · 33rd Mississippi
40th Mississippi · 1st Mississippi Battalion

WALTHALL'S DIVISION Maj. Gen. Edward C. Walthall
Reynold's Brigade Brig. Gen. Daniel H. Reynolds,[4] Col. Henry C. Bunn,[5]
Lt. Col. Morton C. Galloway
4th Arkansas · 9th Arkansas · 25th Arkansas · 1st Arkansas Mounted Rifles (dismounted)
2nd Arkansas Mounted Rifles (dismounted)

Quarles' Brigade Brig. Gen. George D. Johnston
1st Alabama · 17th Alabama · 29th Alabama · 42nd Tennessee · 48th Tennessee
49th Tennessee · 53rd Tennessee · 55th Tennessee

CHEATHAM'S CORPS Maj. Gen. William B. Bate
CLEBURNE'S DIVISION Brig. Gen. James A. Smith
Govan's Brigade Col. Peter V. Green
1st Arkansas · 2nd Arkansas · 5th Arkansas · 6th Arkansas · 7th Arkansas · 8th Arkansas
13th Arkansas · 15th Arkansas · 19th Arkansas · 24th Arkansas · 3rd Confederate

Smith's Brigade Capt. J. R. Bonner
1st Georgia (Volunteers) · 54th Georgia · 57th Georgia · 63rd Georgia

Granbury's Brigade Maj. William A. Ryan[6]
35th Tennessee · 6th Texas · 7th Texas · 10th Texas · 15th Texas · 17th Texas
18th Texas · 24th Texas · 25th Texas · 5th Confederate

Lowrey's Brigade Lt. Col. John F. Smith[7]
3rd Mississippi · 8th Mississippi · 16th Mississippi · 32nd Mississippi

BATE'S DIVISION Col. D. L. Kenan[8]
Tyler's Brigade Maj. W. H. Wilkinson[9]
2nd Tennessee · 10th Tennessee · 15th Tennessee · 20th Tennessee · 30th Tennessee
37th Tennessee · 37th Georgia · 4th Georgia Battalion Sharpshooters

Finley's Brigade Lt. Col. Eli Washburn
1st Florida · 3rd Florida · 4th Florida · 6th Florida · 7th Florida
1st Florida Cavalry (dismounted)

BROWN'S DIVISION Brig. Gen. Roswell S. Ripley[10]
Gist's Brigade Col. Hume R. Field
16th South Carolina · 24th South Carolina · 46th Georgia · 65th Georgia
3rd Georgia Battalion · 2nd Battalion Georgia Sharpshooters

Maney's Brigade Lt. Col. Christopher C. McKinney
1st Tennessee · 8th Tennessee · 16th Tennessee · 27th Tennessee · 28th Tennessee

Strahl's Brigade Col. James D. Tillman
4th Tennessee · 5th Tennessee · 19th Tennessee · 24th Tennessee
31st Tennessee · 33rd Tennessee · 38th Tennessee · 41st Tennessee

Vaughn's Brigade Col. William P. Bishop
11th Tennessee · 12th Tennessee · 13th Tennessee · 29th Tennessee · 47th Tennessee
51st Tennessee · 52nd Tennessee · 154th Tennessee

DEPARTMENT OF NORTH CAROLINA
Gen. Braxton Bragg

HOKE'S DIVISION Maj. Gen. Robert F. Hoke[11]
Clingman's Brigade Col. William S. Devane[12]
8th North Carolina · 31st North Carolina · 51st North Carolina · 61st North Carolina

Kirkland's Brigade Brig. Gen. William W. Kirkland
17th North Carolina · 42nd North Carolina · 66th North Carolina

Hagood's Brigade Brig. Gen. Johnson Hagood[13]
Contingent under Lt. Col. James H. Rion
11th South Carolina · 21st South Carolina · 25th South Carolina · 27th South Carolina
7th South Carolina Battalion

Contingent under Lt. Col. John D. Taylor[14]
1st North Carolina Battalion Heavy Artillery · 9th North Carolina Battalion
36th North Carolina · Adams' Battery, Company D, 13th Battalion North Carolina Light Artillery

Contingent under Maj. William A. Holland
40th North Carolina

Colquitt's Brigade Col. Charles T. Zachry
6th Georgia · 19th Georgia · 23rd Georgia · 27th Georgia · 28th Georgia

North Carolina Junior Reserves Brigade Col. John H. Nethercutt
70th North Carolina (1st North Carolina Junior Reserves) · 71st North Carolina (2nd North
Carolina Junior Reserves) · 72nd North Carolina (3rd North Carolina Junior Reserves)
20th Battalion North Carolina Junior Reserves

HARDEE'S CORPS Lt. Gen. William J. Hardee
TALIAFERRO'S DIVISION Brig. Gen. William B. Taliaferro
Elliott's Brigade Brig. Gen. Stephen Elliott, Jr.[1516]
22nd Georgia Battalion · 28th Georgia Battalion (Bonaud's) · 2nd South Carolina Heavy
Artillery · Hanleiter's Battalion · Gist Guard Artillery

Rhett's Brigade Col. William Butler
1st South Carolina Infantry (Regulars) · 1st South Carolina Heavy Artillery
Lucas' South Carolina Battalion

McLAWS' DIVISION Maj. Gen. Lafayette McLaws
Connor's Brigade Brig. Gen. John D. Kennedy
2nd South Carolina · 3rd South Carolina · 7th South Carolina · 8th South Carolina
15th South Carolina · 20th South Carolina · 3rd South Carolina Battalion

Fiser's Brigade Col. John C. Fiser
1st Georgia Regulars · 2nd Georgia Battalion Reserves · 5th Georgia Reserves
6th Georgia Reserves · 27th Georgia Battalion

Harrion's Brigade Col. George P. Harrison
5th Georgia · 32nd Georgia · 47th Georgia

Hardy's Brigade Col. Washington Hardy
50th North Carolina · 77th North Carolina (7th Senior Reserves)
10th North Carolina Battaliojn

Blanchard's Brigade Brig. Gen. Albert G. Blanchard
1st Battalion South Carolina Reserves · 2nd Battalion South Carolina Reserves
6th Battalion South Carolina Reserves · 7th Battalion South Carolina Reserves
Kay's Company South Carolina Reserves

Battalion Artillery Maj. A. Burnett Rhett
LeGuardeur's Battery · H. M. Stuart's Battery (Beaufort Light Artillery)

CAVALRY COMMAND
Lt. Gen. Wade Hampton

WHEELER'S CORPS Maj. Gen. Joseph Wheeler (Army of Tennessee Cavalry)
HUMES' DIVISION Col. Henry M. Ashby
T. Harrison's Brigade Col. Baxter Smith
3rd Arkansas Cavalry · 4th Tennessee Cavalry · 8th Texas Cavalry · 11th Texas Cavalry

Ashby's Brigade Lt. Col. James H. Lewis
1st Tennessee Cavalry · 2nd Tennessee Cavalry · 5th Tennessee Cavalry
9th Tennessee Battalion Cavalry

ALLEN'S DIVISION Brig. Gen. William W. Allen
Hagan's Brigade Col. D. G. White
1st Alabama Cavalry · 3rd Alabama Cavalry · 9th Alabama Cavalry
12th Alabama Cavalry · 51st Alabama Cavalry · 53rd Alabama Cavalry
24th Alabama Battalion Cavalry

Anderson's Brigade Brig. Gen. Robert H. Anderson
3rd Confederate Cavalry · 8th Confederate Cavalry · 10th Confederate Cavalry
5th Georgia Cavalry

DIBRELL'S DIVISION Brig. Gen. George G. Dibrell
Dibrell's Brigade Col. William S. McLemore
4th Tennessee (McLemore's) Cavalry · 13th Tennessee Cavalry
Shaw's Tennessee Battalion Cavalry

Breckenridge's Brigade (formerly Lewis') Col. W. C. P. Breckenridge
1st Kentucky Cavalry · 2nd Kentucky Cavalry · 9th Kentucky Cavalry · 2nd Kentucky
Mounted Infantry · 4th Kentucky Mounted Infantry · 5th Kentucky Mounted Infantry
6th Kentucky Mounted Infantry · 9th Kentucky Mounted Infantry

BUTLER'S DIVISION Maj. Gen. M. C. Butler,[17] Brig. Gen. Evander M. Law
Young's Brigade Col. Gilbert J. Wright
10th Georgia Cavalry · Cobb's Georgia Legion · Jeff Davis Legion · Phillips' Georgia Legion

Butler's Brigade Brig. Gen. Evander M. Law, Brig. Gen. Thomas M. Logan
4th South Carolina Cavalry · 5th South Carolina Cavalr · 6th South Carolina Cavalry

Horse Artillery
Earle's South Carolina Battery · Hart's (Halsey's) South Carolina Battery

*   *   *

1 *Wounded, March 19*
2 *Arrived at Bentonville on March 20*
3 *Unit was listed at the end of March 1865 in two different commands—Adams' & Lowrey's*
Brigades
4 *Wounded March 19, 1865*
5 *Wounded March 19, 1865*
6 *Arrived at Bentonville on March 20, 1865*
7 *Arrived at Bentonville on March 21, 1865*
8 *Wounded March 19, 1865*
9 *Killed March 19, 1865*
10 *Arrived at Bentonville on March 21, 1865 and Cheatham led the division at Bentonville*
11 *Detached from the Army of Northern Virginia and operating with local units—13th Battalion*
North Carolina Light Artillery (three companies) • North Carolina Junior Reserves (three regiments
and one battalion)
12 *Wounded March 21, 1865*
13 *Two regiments and one battalion Fort Fisher garrison served under Hagood at Bentonville*
14 *Wounded March 19, 1865*
15 *Wounded March 19, 1865*
16 *There is some question and confusion about what artillery battalions were present at Bentonville*
and what battalions and/or batteries were actually there. The ones above are known to have been
there. Please consult some of the suggested readings for a complete list of battalions that might have
been present but no known record or account has surfaced to suggest definitively one way or another.
17 *Ill during the Battle of Bentonville, Law commanded division*

Suggested Reading

THE BATTLE OF BENTONVILLE

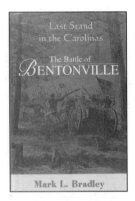

The Battle of Bentonville: Last Stand in the Carolinas
Mark L. Bradley
Savas Publishing, 1996
ISBN-13: 978-1882810-02-4

Not only does Bradley provide the definitive micro-tactical study of the battle of Bentonville, he offers excellent accounts of the fighting at Monroe's Crossroads and Averasboro. Bradley also introduces the reader to the major commanders from both sides. Mark Moore's superb maps complement a lively, accessible narrative built upon primary accounts.

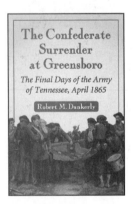

The Confederate Surrender at Greensboro: The Final Days of the Army of Tennessee, April 1865
Robert M. Dunkerly
McFarland, 2013
ISBN-13: 978-0786473-62-5

A month after Bentonville, Joseph Johnston's army finally surrendered in North Carolina. Dunkerly, a recognized expert on the final days of the American Civil War, provides a detailed narrative of the Confederacy's largest surrender. While Robert E. Lee's surrender at Appomattox is more popularly known, Dunkerly's study places the surrender at Greensboro on the same plain as Appomattox.

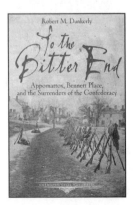

To the Bitter End: Appomattox, Bennett Place, and the Surrenders of the Confederacy
Robert M. Dunkerly
Savas Beatie, 2015
ISBN-13: 978-1611212-52-5

Building on *The Confederate Surrender at Greensboro*, Dunkerly chronicles all of the major Confederate surrenders. His narrative of these events picks up where *Calamity in Carolina* leaves off. Dunkerly authoritatively weaves a story of sometimes-forgotten events, placing each surrender in the overall context of the conclusion of the war.

Moore's Historical Guide to the Battle of Bentonville
Mark A. Moore
Savas Publishing, 1997
ISBN-13: 978-1882810-15-4

Spread out over a wide expanse of terrain, the battle of
Bentonville consisted of complicated maneuvers, with large
forces converging on the field from different directions.
Cartographer Mark Moore breaks down the different
phases of the fighting and tells the story of the battle
through his set of brilliantly constructed maps. An easy-to-
read narrative accompanies each map and gives clarity to
an otherwise confusing battle.

To Prepare for Sherman's Coming:
The Battle of Wise's Forks, March 1865
Wade Sokolosky and Mark Smith
Savas Beatie, 2015
ISBN-13: 978-1611212-66-2

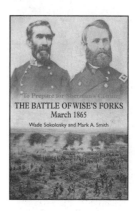

Similar to Monroe's Crossroads, Wise's Forks has been
overshadowed by the larger battles of Averasboro and
Bentonville. Mark Smith and Wade Sokolosky, authorities
on the Civil War in North Carolina, have filled a gap in the
story of the Carolinas campaign. Their narrative covers
the critical operation of the Federal attempt to establish
and secure a supply base for William Tecumseh Sherman's
armies and the efforts of the Confederates to thwart them.

The Battle of Monroe's Crossroads and the Civil War's
Last Campaign
Eric Wittenberg
Savas Beatie, 2006
ISBN-13: 978-1932714-17-3

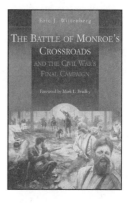

Eric Wittenberg, a long-recognized expert on cavalry
operations in the Civil War, chronicles an oft-forgotten
engagement during the Carolinas campaign. Wittenberg
not only brings Monroe's Crossroads to life, but discusses
its overall impact on the cavalry in future operations. The
appendices are invaluable, with Wittenberg addressing the
controversies surrounding the battle.

About the Authors

Daniel Davis is the chief historian for Emerging Civil War. He is a graduate of Longwood University with a B.A. in Public History. Dan has worked as a historian at both Appomattox Court House National Historic Site and at the Fredericksburg and Spotsylvania National Military Park. He resides in Fredericksburg, Virginia, with his wife Katy and Beagle mix, Bayla.

Phill Greenwalt graduated from George Mason University with a M.A. in American History and also has a B.A. in history from Wheeling Jesuit University. He is currently a historian with the National Park Service at George Washington Birthplace National Monument and Thomas Stone National Historic Site. He started with the National Park Service as a historical interpreter intern at Fredericksburg and Spotsylvania National Military Park. He currently resides in the historic Northern Neck of Virginia with his wife, Adel.

Dan and Phill are co-authors of *Bloody Autumn: The Shenandoah Valley Campaign of 1864* and *Hurricane from the Heavens: The Battle of Cold Harbor*. Both are also regular contributors to Emerging Civil War, and Dan serves as the site's managing editor. <www.emergingcivilwar.com>